Aerocene

SKIRA

Hans Ulrich Obrist
in Conversation with
Tomás Saraceno

On Aerocene

HUO   When did *Aerocene* start, and how many years does it encompass?

TS   The term *Aerocene* came about after an invitation from Bruno Latour and Bronislaw Szerszynski, when they asked us to propose an Anthropocene Monument. We responded to the invitation with the idea to invent a new epoch that would be the chance to shape a period of time, together, and that could also help us to frame future projects, such as *Cloud Cities* and *Air-Port-City.*

I always dreamed of floating among the clouds, but how to do it? As an artist, I thought we could start by building a flying museum. In 2007, with a community of people from all over the world, we started collecting used plastic bags. These were then washed, cut, and pasted together to create a large envelope full of air. When the sun rises over the horizon and the air inside the envelope heats up, the museum floats in the sky. Seeing it floating for the first time was a magical moment. That project is still a miracle for me, that just by taping together the plastic bags we throw away so quickly, one can do something so fascinating with them.

Only a few people have experimented with this simple physics in the past. When I was at NASA in 2009 for a residency, people could not believe that you can use such elemental technologies to float. I met an astronaut back then who has been to space many times, and he promised that the next flight he wants to do is with *Aerocene.* The project proposes a radical change in how we could be up in the air, and how we can imagine ourselves moving towards new futures.

We wanted to imagine a new epoch, one that could leave behind the subjugation of the Anthropocene. We called it *Aerocene*: a period of ecological awareness, in which we learn together to float, live in the air and reach an ethical commitment to the atmosphere and the earth.

The idea of *Aerocene* as an epoch also refers to Felix Guattari's book *The Three Ecologies.* Guattari talks not only about the "environmental" ecology, but also the mental and social ecologies, which are all needed to achieve global change. So, we came up with activities that would allow us to dream together—*Museo Aero Solar* is one, a flying museum to rehearse the ways we experience the planet. Now for example, in the context of a collaboration with Exhibition Road in London, we are working on the *Aerocene Explorer,* a kit that allows anyone to sense the atmosphere in different ways through this experience.

HUO   So is *Aerocene* a balloon?

TS   Well, we think of *Aerocene* as the time when we will finally be able to transcend the Anthropocene. At the same time, it is an artistic project, and the balloons are in fact sculptures, which float quite differently to any other balloon.

The way the sculptures float depends on just a few degrees of difference in temperature between the air they contain and the air outside. To take off, you fill the sculpture with air and the sun heats it up until it starts to float. On August 27, 2016 we launched a sculpture called *Aerocene Gemini* from Berlin and it reached the north of Poland. It traveled for 800 kilometers without using a drop of fuel, just thanks to the temperature differential, without solar panels, batteries or burners!

So one can also think of *Aerocene* as a way of making these slight variations in temperature tangible. The "two degrees" have become a central point in the climate change debate, but they are quite difficult to perceive otherwise.

I think this is quite in tune with Timothy Morton and his theory on hyper-objects and how things become alive. In this case, the sculptures get lifted into the air by the heat of the sun.

HUO   What do you mean by the statement "from the Anthropocene to *Aerocene*"?

TS   *Aerocene* is an invitation to move away from the current anthropocentric and earth-focused points of view. Instead of looking towards the past – the way geological epochs are usually defined – we are experimenting by speculating about an age that has not yet begun, that you cannot yet perceive. In a way, we are trying to anticipate the stratigraphy of the future, by looking at the atmosphere as a more-than-geological layer.

Aerocene is also a way of re-examining freedom of movement between countries. Ultimately, the air belongs to everyone. We want to imagine a new infrastructure to facilitate the movement of people, which could bypass the increasingly hard and rigid infrastructures that exist today.

HUO   I remember when you were a student at the IUAV, when Stefano Boeri and I were teaching. You arrived on the first day and you had this epiphany to create a habitable layer over the railway station and an entire neighborhood, to do something not on the scale of a sculpture, but something on the scale of a city. And here, we are going back to that scale in a way. Perhaps this was the beginning of *Aerocene*?

TS   Yes. I am always thinking about the fact that we know how to float in the water, but not (yet) how to float in the air. Of course, Venice is built over water, so when I was living there I started to imagine if it could be possible to learn to build in the air just like we learned to build on water. It is possible to be in the air with very simple, elemental forces. We always talk about aerodynamics and not aerostatics. Aerostatic forces mean that it is possible to defy gravity and dance and weave across the different strata of the atmosphere.

If we begin to think in terms of aerostatics, we get a completely different sense of our position as a species within the planetary system.

HUO   Can we actually say that *Aerocene* is maybe Biosphere 3?

TS   Yes [laughing]. You know that Biosphere 2 failed, but it is still urgent to keep experimenting. We need to study more closed systems in order to understand the mutual relationships and co-dependency between all forms of life. Perhaps Biosphere 3 will be floating in the air, like Biosphere 1 – planet Earth.

We are making steps towards it. We did an experiment that became a worldwide record: we flew a couple of people with a certified vehicle, without burning any fossil fuels from the beginning of the journey to the end. This had never been done before.

HUO   A fully solar-powered flight. Can you tell me about this? It is a world premiere right? So when did that happen?

TS   On November 8, 2015 at White Sands National Monument in New Mexico. It was quite amazing, as it's close to a militarized space… White Sands is where the first atomic bomb detonation was conducted by the US Army in 1945. As a result of the explosion, a cloud of radioactive particles spread all around the planet. For this reason, the event is being considered one of the markers of the Anthropocene. In a sense, it was the perfect symbolic place to leave one age and enter into a new one. Some of the sand there has crystallized and turned into glass – which makes me think again about Timothy Morton, and the idea of a latent state of things, how they can change state when they acquire temperature.

At White Sands, the D-OAEC *Aerocene* sculpture was able to lift a person in the air using only the irradiation of the sun as an energy source. As the sun rose, we also rose, silently and slowly, without explosions and without fuel. We felt as if gravity was inverted, no longer pushing us towards the center of the Earth, but towards the Universe.

HUO   Kiel Moe has described you as "envisioning an entirely different thermodynamic model for living in this century." I once spoke to Ilya Prigogine in an interview about the second law of thermodynamics and of course about the notion of entropy. So I suppose what Biosphere 2 proposed is a different model than entropy, because in a way this model of a closed circuit, will actually prevent entropy from happening.

TS   We have been working with the French National Space Agency (CNES), which in the 1970s began an experimental program using this passive way of flying for meteorological observation. We are working together to test an unrealized future, using this method.

The long-range aerosolar sculptures can float around the globe for several weeks without any batteries, burners, helium. During the day they stand at 40 km of altitude (space starts at 100 km) heated by the sun. Then at night they drop down to around 20 km, staying afloat by picking up the infrared radiation from the Earth. They make a kind of thermodynamic choreography, 40 km, to 20 km, to 40 km, to 20 km.

HUO   So they move across waves, with highs, lows and intervals, pauses and silence.

TS   Exactly. Working with the CNES engineers we speculate that theoretically it is possible for such a balloon to stay in the air for up to three years, floating around the world many times. *Aerocene* is a way of sensing the dynamics of the air.

On Earth, batteries and solar panels cause a lot of problems, such as disposal, recycling, lifespan… considering the Earth itself as a battery, thanks to the latent heat it absorbs during the day, can solve these. The radiation travels up to the stratosphere, and in our case, reaches the bottom part of the sculpture and keeps it afloat.

Perhaps we even need to redefine the concept of orbit. Today orbits begin at 160 km, which is the altitude at which a powered object can escape gravity and stop falling down. But aerosolar objects somehow resist gravity by utilizing the power of the sun to travel around the planet. What are the orbital limits of *Aerocene*? Once you move beyond planetary boundaries, a space for cosmic imagination opens up. Humans very rarely have a chance to move in such a different, almost alien way, and we don't know which new ideas and modes of thinking might emerge.

Have you ever flown in a balloon?

HUO   No. But I have heard a lot of accounts of flying in balloons… Do you know the Swedish/English architect Ralph Erskine? He was one of the members of the Team Ten, with Peter and Alison Smithson, and also Aldo van Eyck. Ralph Erskine tried to develop cities for the Antarctic, and he was also obsessed with balloons! Whenever he signed, he would write "Ralph Erskine" and then he would draw a hot air balloon! [laughing]. Anyway, no, I have never been in a balloon.

TS   Yes, Erskine would use balloons as a symbol of optimism, for a better way of moving and being. To be in a balloon is a beautiful experience. The substantial difference between a normal aerostatic balloon and the sculptures we build, lies in their mode of floating in the air. And what is amazing is that if you look down at Earth, you can see the trees shaking wildly, but up in the air, everything is still. If you were talking to someone who was also floating with you in an open basket, you would see that their hair would not be moving at all, not even one millimeter. It takes some time for your brain to process this crazy phenomenon…

HUO   It is a conundrum!
TS   This is what we describe as stillness in motion.

HUO   We could call it "dynamic stillness."
TS   Or "aerostatic speed," as opposed to the usual aerodynamic movement. I also always think of the so-called overview effect – the cognitive shift that astronauts have reported feeling after viewing Earth from space. The concept that you have to go to the moon or outer space to feel and sense the planet, its scale… the Earth as a planetary system in which we are entangled.

HUO   Indeed, the planetary, or even extra-planetary perspective has always been a motivation for you. Thinking about the almost unlimited applications of *Aerocene,* what is your ultimate ambition for the *Aerocene* project? Where are these unrealized parts of your *Aerocene* dreams?
TS   The ultimate ambition of *Aerocene* would be to manifest a series of clouds large enough to support entire cities in the sky. In this way, you could build a floating biosphere – Biosphere 3 – a closed system that would allow us to live with understanding of our own, terrestrial biosphere and the amazing level of co-dependency of its components. In parallel, a Mission Planet Earth program to study Earth's biosphere, and at the same time carry out research on human life support systems, towards floating futures.

On the way to this goal, *Aerocene* seeks to activate this way of thinking. We are always already floating, on a cosmic scale, within the infinitely complex and interconnected cosmic web. *Aerocene,* and the way of moving that it provokes, is a way of tuning our awareness, not just to meteorological cloud formations, but to galactic clouds and nebulae. Relating to the interplanetary scale could help us reach a broader perspective on this planet, via sun-enabled performative action, which makes this way of being tangible.

It is about moving into a connected way of thinking and being together. Thinking about how we can rearticulate the level of engagement in the epoch we live in, *Aerocene* moves away from the Anthropocene and the big decisions made by only the few. How can we become part of another, new epoch, where the decision-making is more distributed? *Aerocene* can encourage us to be pro-active in shifting the discourse, not so much about the 1% versus the 99%, but rather us wilfully becoming part of something, as opposed to having it thrust upon us.

HUO   One thing I was also wondering, if you think about the ultimate idea of the *Aerocene,* to what extent is it a production of collective intelligence? How can people participate in your *Aerocene* project? How they can contribute ideas to your open system?

TS   What we are doing at the moment is expanding the conversation of *Aerocene* and this incorporates the social aspect of the project, which we like to think of in the terms – if 'I' Anthropocene, then 'we' Aerocene.

Together with MIT and the Department of Earth, Atmospheric and Planetary Sciences, we are continually working on the Aerocene Float Predictor. This is a program that can plot the trajectories of *Aerocene* sculptures using real-time wind forecasting data from the NOAA Global Forecast System. I believe the Float Predictor expands the public imagination regarding the potential of *Aerocene.* This tool is imagined in a virtual space for the *Aerocene* epoch, not just to predict where the sculptures will land, but also to encourage people to be more aware of the planet, its cycles and its ecologies. Recently, Christiana Figueres, the former Executive Secretary of the United Nations

Framework Convention on Climate Change, used the Float Predictor to travel back home. These trajectories become drawings made with the wind, signatures to declare the Day of Independence from Fossil Fuels.

What is also encouraging is what we are doing with the *Aerocene Explorer*. We are working with a lot of different communities from balloonists to radio amateurs, using all sorts of do-it-together technology. An *Aerocene Campus* with Exhibition Road in London was organized, an event that saw the participation of a very diverse group of people, from sociologists to philosophers.

Together with Public Lab and one of their researchers Nick Shapiro, we are quite keen to find ways of attaching new devices and sensors to the sculptures. He is a specialist in air pollution monitoring, so during our last float from Berlin to Poland, he put filters on the sculptures to try to see which particles were in the air and then, with a microscope, he could look at the type of pollution in the air.

Aerocene sculptures could be an amazing way of being with life in the air, such as spiders that reach an altitude of up to 6 kilometers, or the tardigrades that have been found on the solar wings of the International Space Station.

HUO   When did you discover the unlimited potential of *Aerocene*? Do you remember the day?

TS   Not exactly… [laughing]. One of the key moments was when I met Dominic Michaelis. He was a great architect based in Toulon, and a friend of Buckminster Fuller… and after meeting Gyula Kosice, we started to speculate about all these relationships between social, political and economic systems.

HUO   The artist Gyula Kosice was an inspiration for you, an influence from Argentina, perhaps because of his utopic, almost cosmic kind of architecture. What was his early influence on you?

TS   At the time I was studying architecture, Gyula was proposing a completely different approach to what architecture could be, also on a completely different scale. For instance, he would describe spaces in his hydrospatial cities. He would also come up with ideas like a space for cosmic meditation, a space for the transcendence of being. He had a speculative vision about what architecture could do, be and propose. He was speculative also in terms of social and political challenges.

For example, when somebody asks where I'm from, I always try to reply that I am from planet Earth. My answer corresponds to how I feel today on this planet.

HUO	You describe the *Aerocene* project as a symbiotic relationship with the Earth, the sun, and also of course with humans. Can you tell me more about this symbiotic research?

TS	We have looked at the history of energy systems and the so-called socio-metabolic regimes – the idea that the transition from agrarian societies to industrial ones rests on a shift from solar-based sources of energy to geological sources (coal and later oil). The sociologist Bronislaw Szerszynski has written that *Aerocene* could be the vision for a new transition – inhabiting the atmosphere using the energy of the sun and of the wind.

HUO	And how is your spider-related work linked to the *Aerocene* project?

TS	There is a social spider species called the *Stegodyphus* that moves using a method called "ballooning." Together, they launch a web of silk threads into the air, which are picked up by the wind, allowing the spiders to fly for hundreds of kilometers sometimes. It is an amazing collaborative phenomenon that represents a completely different way of using thermodynamic flows, which was a great inspiration for us when we were conceptualizing *Aerocene.*

But more generally, the spider work, *Aerocene,* and many of my other works, are about making visible and tangible what is latent, whether it be a spider web or the jet streams in the stratosphere.

HUO	It seems we are living in quite a politically dystopic age. Perhaps your work shows us a way out of this dystopia, and that art is perhaps a principle of hope. Regarding utopias and dystopias you say "something that is impossible for some species, is possible for others, something that is a utopian idea for someone who does not know how to conceive or achieve it might already have been accomplished by others." It is interesting then to question the relativity of utopia as some utopic ideas are quite concrete. What is your definition of utopia?

TS   I would say that dystopia is a nightmare, while utopia is like a dream you want to accomplish. It is a physiological necessity to sleep and dream. Every human being spends one third of their life in a state of sleep, in a psychological realm. To have a balanced relationship, we also need nightmares to compare with dreams. Utopia, for me, is the courage to have these moments of illumination about what one wants to pursue. But it is also about how we can dream together and take responsibility to share a dream.

HUO   Can you talk more about mobility and the idea of moving?

TS   Currently, we move horizontally, but we can imagine a vertical mobility, an aerography of winding trajectories that takes you to different parts of the atmosphere, bending between the troposphere and the stratosphere. I'm thinking, for example, of a project we are working on called *Sunny Day*. In Berlin, there are three months in the year when the clouds are very low in the skies over the city. We are thinking about a sculpture that floats up vertically so that people can reach their sunny day. What interests me is to investigate this kind of three-dimensional world. Of course, one cannot forget how the sun affects people psychologically.

HUO   Did you hear about James Bridle's work? He developed *Cloud Index,* a digital commission, which is fascinating. It is based on networks that connect to clouds.

TS   Interesting. In 1802, the amateur meteorologist Luke Howard wrote an essay titled *On the Modifications of Clouds* – which he presented at the Askesian Society in London – where he first came up with a classification system for the clouds above our heads. He always named the clouds in a state of becoming: from stratus to nimbus stratus. He embedded in the name itself the future temporality of these bodies. This is once again the idea of a latent state; the way of describing something is also its way of becoming.

HUO   And since the beginning of time, humans have always looked upwards to the sky. As James Bridle said, to determine the future today we look at the clouds. Do you agree with this statement "If we wish to change the future we must change the weather"?

TS   The weather in a political sense? I do agree. I would say that to change the atmosphere, you have to change the weather of politics and ways of being. I participated in a conference on geo-engineering at IASS Potsdam, on the topic of generating new clouds by reflecting on how particles are spread. Clouds can have different albedo – reflectivity – depending on their different size and density, and they could form sheds to cool the planet. And there I said, well, we could also float humans up into the air, above the clouds! It sounds like the reversal of a geo-engineering fix, and this might be the way in which we can also reconnect with the weather. *Aerocene* doesn't ask the Earth to change, instead we become one with the weather.

HUO   When you look at your earlier practice, a lot of what is later to come is already included in these first works. In one of your first works, when you were at Städelschule, you were already making these "Foam" conversations.

TS   Do you remember my installation *On Space Time Foam* that was formed from three large layers of a transparent membrane that visitors could climb onto? If I move in the installation, then you move, and so on. The butterfly effect becomes much more tangible. Space-time is similar, it is a fabric. Depending on its mass, an object can curve space and time. One can think about it like this: when two people are very close in an inflatable environment there is a pull between them that pushes them into a kind of social black hole. So, our spatial perception changes and with it, our perception of space-time as well. With *On Space Time Foam* we wanted to turn it into something that is perceivable, because, if someone is standing in the membrane above, the distance for you to walk from one point to another bends, and space ceases to exist.

It played on spaces of reverberation and how things are interconnected in spaces of coexistence.

HUO   One thing I wanted to ask you about is the notion of the "hyperobject." The history of art from the nineteenth century to the 1950s and '60s, was far more and above all a history of objects. Then Lucy Lippard and many others started to talk about the dematerialization of art in the 1960s, so an art of non-objects. In the '90s, there was a lot of discussion about Michel Serres' notion of the quasi-object. The football is the ultimate example of the quasi-object, in the sense that it only gains meaning from the complex web around it, but if you don't use the football it does not really have meaning in a way. In this sense, we have objects, quasi-objects, and non-objects.

TS   And latent objects!

HUO   Exactly, that is very nicely rephrased; the quasi-objects of Michel Serres are kind of latent objects. And then, we enter the age of the Anthropocene, and that is where Timothy Morton enters and he is such an inspiration for many artists. Because we enter the age of the hyperobjects, and these would be things like climate or the weather, bigger phenomena. The first time I was made aware of this was at the memorial of my friend Felix Gonzalez-Torres and Roni Horn said, "Felix is the weather. His medium is the weather." Then I read Timothy Morton and obviously your work is somehow – I mean – you make objects, quasi objects, non-objects – but you do engage far more with hyperobjects, so I wanted to ask you more about that and about your interest in Timothy Morton.

TS   For me it is something really personal: when I was a child, I would have nightmares about not being able to count, for example. Somebody would give me the task of having to count all the sand grains on planet Earth, and I would wake up thinking "Oh, this is impossible!" Timothy talks about this spectrum of knowing, this idea that black matter represents 95 % of all that is yet to be named. I am pushed to speculate on the 95 % that might be there. We only fully understand the gravitational pull of how things might come together, but we still do not know what it is that makes us come together, when gravity is not there anymore. Morton works through these multiple scales and approaches, which I also love to do. I also relate to Markus J. Buehler and his *Biomateriomics,* an attempt to understand the merging properties of different phenomena and systems that might correlate and overlap at the same time, moving from one to the other. I always think that we are locked into certain systems, and with *Aerocene* we are trying to see if a presence in art might also be a presence in parallel worlds. From art to science, to cosmology… or whatever it may be.

HUO   Like parallel realities, you mean, like in quantum physics.

TS   Yes.

HUO   Very last question. Rainer Maria Rilke wrote this little book *Letters to a Young Poet* and – this is one of my recurring questions. Now that you have so much experience, what would be your advice to a young artist?

TS   To get lost! It is beautiful to get lost. Then you will find the way, but before you do, you have to get lost somehow.

Eva Horn

Aesthetics of the Air

Tomás Saraceno's Aerocene

What is air? We breathe it, we feel it, we travel in it, we are touched by it. Googling it takes you to the "atmosphere of the Earth," i.e. the layer of gases surrounding the planet. It informs you about the chemistry of air: 78.09 % nitrogen, 20.95 % oxygen, 0.93 % argon, 0.04 % carbon dioxide – 0.04 % and counting, one could add. Moreover, a variable amount of water vapor, causing the dryness or humidity of air depending on the location and weather conditions. Then there is pollution of course; smoke, dust, pollen, gases, chemicals. We breathe and feel that too, or not. It actually takes new and unprecedented levels of industrial pollution in cities like Beijing, Delhi or Riyadh to feel and see the profound alteration that modern life has brought upon the air, a substance so basic to all life on Earth that we are hardly ever aware of it.

Seen this way, air is a chemical formula, a complex scientific object – *a matter of fact.* Yet, be it in the form of pollution or rising CO_2 levels, the air is also one of the biggest environmental problems we are facing today. It is thus *a matter of concern,* of political debate and human decision-making. Even if in the past decades we have improved our models and simulations on the chemistry and behavior of the Earth's atmosphere, the object "air," or that which today is most often called "climate" or "atmosphere" remains elusive, both as a matter of fact and concern. Equally elusive or "wicked" are the conflicts over which political steps to take, as the air transcends the traditional instances of political decision-making, such as in municipalities or nations. Following Timothy Morton, one could say that the air is a "hyperobject" that challenges both scientific conceptualization and proper politicization. It is "massively distributed in time and space relative to humans" and an object we cannot really view from a distance – except from the uninhabitable position of outer space. In fact, there is no meta-perspective or meta-language that could create a viewpoint of "neutral" observation or experimentation on the air: we are permanently engulfed by it, penetrated, transcended and transformed by it. The air involves us when we are already always involved with it, with every breath and every airplane we take.

"The air, the air is everywhere …," they sang back in the hippie days when we used to think air pollution was the only thing that was wrong with

Bruno Latour, *We have never been modern* (trans. C. Porter), Boston: Harvard University Press, 1993.

Timothy Morton, *Hyperobjects. Philosophy and Ecology After the End of the World,* Minneapolis: University of Minnesota Press, 2013: 1.

This is the song "Air" from the musical *Hair* (1967).

it.| Air is the medium we live in, together with all other living creatures — *a medium of life.* For media are not just tools for communication or data processing, the media are, more elementally, "vessels and environments, containers of possibility that anchor our existence and make what we are doing possible."|

John Durham Peters, *The Marvelous Clouds. Toward a Philosophy of Elemental Media,* Chicago / London: University of Chicago Press, 2015: 2.

Elements of nature, such as air, climate, the ozone layer, fire, water, or soil are not just the material basis of life; they are its *conditions of possibility.* Not just of biological life, but also of life in a cognitive and social sense.

Just as with any other medium, the air remains in the background of our perception as long as it functions without disruption, friction or corruption. Because and only to the extent that it is transparent, invisible, permeable, and gaseous, the air is a medium. As soon as it steps into the foreground — in the form of storms, mustard gas clouds, an overload of dust and aerosols, or the utter lack of air — life itself is threatened. "The background," Peter Sloterdijk writes, "only breaks its silence when foreground processes exceed its burdening capacity. How many real ecological and military disasters were needed before it could be said with juristic, physical and atmotechnic precision how one can set up humanely breathable air environments?"| With pollution, changing

Peter Sloterdijk, *Spheres,* vol. 3: *Foams* (trans. W. Hoban), South Pasadena: Semiotext(e), 2016: 63.

weather patterns, extreme weather events and other consequences of global warming, the silent, imperceptible background has stepped to the forefront of our attention and our concerns — be they scientific, social, or political.

How can we conceive of this fragile yet existential being in the air as a specific aspect or way of being in the world? How can we experience it and maybe explore it without messing with it, as we do now? The current scientific definition of air as the composition and behavior of the Earth's atmosphere does not really help here. It reduces air to matter that can merely be researched with the signature distance of the scientific gaze. Science "objectifies" the elusive and complicated phenomenalism of our media of life by precisely robbing them of their mediality and reducing them to a fixed, discernable, if extremely complex object of investigation.

As a complement and critical reflection of the scientific take on air and climate, what we need to grasp are the ways in which *the air acts as a medium.* A medium to the manifold forms of being alive, of being in an environment,

     Eva Horn

and of being social. We need to recover the phenomenological dimension of "being in the air," the ways humans perceive and handle the medium they live in and live by. This includes the ways we breathe it, feel it on our skin, sweat and shiver, notice the smells and changes of the seasons, our perceptions and uses of different atmospheres, and eventually the politics of the bubbles and pockets of air that we inhabit. What does it mean to "inhabit the air"?|

Bronislaw Szerzsynski, "Up", *Aerocene* newspaper, Berlin: Studio Tomás Saraceno, 2015: 15.

How can we explore the interconnectedness of bodies, environments, social structures, and individual human experiences made possible by the air? Science has a tendency to sever the ties that bind the medium of life to the living itself. It discounts the experiences and interactions living organisms have within and of this medium, as subjects of perception and of affect, as metabolic organisms and ultimately as social beings.

What we need is a way of re-thinking the *mediality* of air, of climate, and of weather beyond or as a complement to the confines of a scientific approach. This means to go beyond abstractions such as "global temperatures," beyond statistical accounts of "general changing weather patterns," and eventually also beyond the handy solutions of so-called "green technol-

Bronislaw Szerszynski, "Reading and writing the weather: climate technics and the moment of responsibility" *Theory, Culture and Society*, 2010, vol. 27 (2–3): 9–30.

ogy."| Maybe it is not just all about a politico-technological fix. Thinking about the air as a medium of life would mean seeing air not only as a predicament of *nature*, but also of *culture*, as a Latourian "hybrid" that engages both in matters of fact and matters of concern. Tomás Saraceno's installations and environments explore this crucial yet blurry zone of transfer between a scientific approach to nature, and a hybrid, experimental and phenomenologically more open take on the elements of life, such as the sun, the air, the ground, the spaces we live in, the atmospheres we are creating.

Historically, air has always been such a hybrid. This is why it makes sense not to just wait for the latest findings of climatology and Earth Systems Science to get a grasp on it. It makes sense to delve into a genealogy of older, seemingly outdated ways of thinking about the air in a very elemental way. We find a type of "hybrid" knowledge that does not separate natural conditions from social forms, bodies and minds from the places they dwell. It starts with a much richer definition of the air, mainly as a synonym for "climate,"

  Aesthetics of the Air

sometimes even for "environment," in a given location. This is, for example, the topic of one of the earliest treatises in medicine, Hippocrates' *On Airs, Waters, and Places*. "Whoever wishes to investigate medicine properly" Hippocrates writes, "should … consider the seasons of the year, and what effects each of them produces, for they are not at all alike, … Then the winds, the hot and the cold, especially such as are common to all countries, and then such as are peculiar to each locality." The treatise offers a theory of the influences of the "air," here actually a shorthand for multiple different climatic factors such as winds, air quality, the nature of the soil, humidity, and seasonal weather patterns. Human life is perceived as intricately bound to what today we would call "environmental conditions": climate, water quality, staple foods, and soils. These elements shape the bodies and mentalities of the inhabitants in a given location. From Antiquity well into the age of Enlightenment, humans have been marked and formed by the places they dwell in, the *topoi*.

Previously air was a synonym for climate. The word "climate," derived from κλίνειν (to lean, rest, recline, bend) actually meant "local conditions" and was originally a purely geographical term: a position defined by the inclination of the sun, the latitude. This "air" or "climate" define, in Ancient thought, the living conditions at a specific location (a *topos*). (A thing such as "global climate," which cannot be felt or observed phenomenologically, would not have made any sense). Forming life in a given place, however, the air not only influences the body but also the mentalities, emotions and beliefs, and ultimately the social institutions of its inhabitants. For a long time, the theory of cultures and cultural differences was actually a theory about the differences between climates and livelihoods in different climatic zones. Hot climes, the argument goes, produce different cultures, religions, and forms of power than cold or temperate zones. "Air" here is a predicament that links individuals, bodies, metabolisms, mentalities, social institutions, and political forms. Certain climates create certain bodily conditions, which in turn call for specific cultural and social institutions, be it laws, forms of government, the organization of work, or of the relationship between the sexes. The air creates societies by calling for specific forms of social bonds. The link between climate and society does not necessarily need to be thought of as a form of determinism (as it often has, though), but maybe rather, as the 18th century philosopher Johann Gottlieb Herder put it, as a certain "pull" towards specific forms of social life. Climate creates a cultural and anthropological disposition: "The climate does not force, but inclines," Herder puns.| Johann Gottlieb Herder, *Outlines of a Philosophy of the History of Man* (trans. T. Churchill), London: printed for J. Johnson, by Luke Hansard, 1800: 176. He is also one of the first thinkers to point out that humans are not only influenced by climate, but they in turn, also transform landscapes and local climates. Culture starts with elementary cultural techniques such as agriculture and canalization that change landscapes and climates profoundly: "Once, Europe was a dank forest; and other regions … were the same. Forests are now exposed to the rays of the Sun; and the inhabitants themselves have changed with the climate. … We may consider humankind, therefore, as a band of bold though diminutive giants, gradually descending from the mountains to subjugate the earth and climates with their feeble arms. How far they are capable of going in this respect, futurity will show."| Herder, *Outlines*:176. Human cultures are, as it were, in a feedback loop with climate: by changing the climate, humankind changes itself. *Dwelling* in the air means coming together as living beings, being formed and transformed by weather, winds, seasons, and temperatures. Cultures, in turn, must be understood as forms of *working the air*, transforming it into a habitable, productive, even exploitable resource, or destroying it and making it unlivable.

Yet, *dwelling* in the climate is not the only way of being in the air. Alongside ancient theories of climate as a theory linking locations and societies, there is the tradition of thinking about the "meteors," the emanations of air floating in space between the Earth and the moon. While "climate" indicates a locality, "meteorology" as defined by Aristotle deals with the evanescent, unpredictable flow and dynamics of air – such as comets, clouds, winds, hail, and thunderstorms.| Aristotle, *Meteorologica* (trans. E. W. Webster), *The Works of Aristotle*, vol. III, Oxford: Clarendon Press, 1931. Μετέωρος (meteoros) means "floating," "lofty," "raised up high." *Meteorology* thus does not look at given states and regularities, but at flowing singularities, which are not subject to fixed rules of nature: the exhalations and emanations of the air, things floating in it (e.g. clouds, boreal fires), and flows of movement (e.g. wind). Meteors, for Aristotle, are transient mixtures of the elements of fire, water, and earth, with and inside the fourth element: air.| The meteorological approach to the medium air focuses not on states and locations but on flows, i.e. on the δύναμις, the *power* or *energy* of the air. Here, air is not so much an environment but a system of fluxes, forces and events, a conveyor belt of movement and transport. A medium of energy.

As such, the air is the ever-moving carrier of the seeds of life. Alexander von Humboldt calls the atmosphere an "aerial ocean (in German: "Luft-ozean") in which we are submerged." He is the first to chart air's thermic states as they depart from the system of latitudes in his famous map of the "isotherms" of 1838. For the meteorological view, life floats and hovers in the air in the form of "fertilizing dust or pollen," "seeds of plants," "eggs of insects" and microorganisms.| "Even on the polar ice the air resounds with the cries or songs of birds, and with the hum of insects. Nor is it only the lower dense and vaporous strata of the atmosphere which are thus filled with life, but also the higher and more ethereal regions,"| Humboldt writes. The 18th and 19th centuries would speak of climates as *"circumfusa"*: that which flows around organisms, engulfs and transports the bodies of living beings, be it plants, animals or humans in an ever-flowing, ever-changing medium.|

Humboldt, "Physiognomy of Plants": 227.

Alexander von Humboldt, "Physiognomy of Plants", in *Aspects of Nature. Different Lands and Different Climates* (trans. Mrs. Sabine), Philadelphia: Lea and Blanchard, 1848: 228.

Jean-Baptiste Fressoz, "Circonvenir les circumfusa. La chimie, l'hygiénisme et la libéralisation des 'choses environnantes,' France, 1750–1850", *Revue d'histoire moderne & contemporaine,* 56–4, Octobre–Décembre 2009.

Even a brief genealogy of knowledge on airs and climates hints at an age-old insight into their *mediality.* This mediality, however, has been forgotten and actively erased by both the modern concept of scientific meteorology, and the equally modern separation between social and natural conditions. Yet, seen as a *medium of life,* air binds together and sustains human bodies, locations, cultures, societies, and environments. Air is a state that shapes and lends stability to the living organism, and it provides a primary source of energy. Air is also a system of fluxes and pressures, creating life in a system of movements. Air is thus both a medium of location or sustenance (climate), and of transport or transmission (meteors). It is in this duality of air that we may find the elements for a phenomenology of being in the air or, as it were, a "spherology."|

Peter Sloterdijk's *Spheres* project, especially vol. III.

What does it mean to *explore the air* besides measuring its chemistry? It would mean, as Peter Sloterdijk has suggested, an "explication" of the air –

taking it from an imperceptible background of our existence into the bright light of testing it, remodeling it, disrupting it, playing or experimenting with it. In the modern age, atmospheres have been made "explicit" by being artificially altered, e.g. by creating closed, climate-controlled atmospheres in greenhouses or shopping malls, or by destroying breathable air in gas warfare or death chambers. Air conditioning, chemical warfare, artificial biospheres, domed cities, even terraforming and climate engineering can be seen as more or less demonic, more or less phantasmal ways of understanding the air, by altering, reconstructing, or destroying it as a medium of life. Atmospheres, Sloterdijk argues, "had to become unbreathable for people to learn to recognize them-selves as guardians, reconstructors or reinventors of what had merely been taken for granted." Often enough, we have learned to understand and conceptualize the functions of the medium of air precisely by disrupting it.

What would it mean to "explicate" the air experimentally? Maybe the global-scale experiment of anthropogenic climate change and environmental disruption that has come to be called the "Anthropocene" can be seen as such an explication. By altering the composition and flow systems of the air and water, humankind has ultimately engaged in the *total explication of air* as the medium of life. It does so by precisely testing the limits of its very mediality. How long will the air endure the alteration of its complex, yet seemingly infinitely resilient nature? At what point will the medium of life cease to be one? If the Anthropocene is an almost demonic way of explicating the air on a global scale (and maybe of all other elements, too) there may also be differ-ent, less "total" and less demonic strategies in experimentation. On the one hand, there are the more or less utopian or pragmatic "techno-fixes" – from mitigating climate change by environmental policy, to trying to reverse it by direct climate engineering (e.g. through sulfur injections). In this mode, humans cast themselves as masters and stewards of nature, adjusting their iron grasp on it in the name of "sustainability," "green economy," "climate mitigation" etc. Here, the Anthropocene is seen as fulfilling or transcending the elemen-tary gesture of modernity: to assert human freedom as domination over, or as liberation from the constraints of nature, yet with a certain "respect" towards

Eva Horn, "Air conditioning. Taming the Climate as a Dream of Civilization," in James Graham (ed.), *Climates: Architecture and the Planetary Imaginary,* Zürich / New York: Lars Müller Publishers, 2016.

Peter Sloterdijk, *Spheres,* vol. 3: *Foams* (trans. W. Hoban), South Pasadena: Semiotext(e), 2016: 63.

Among the most vocal proponents of a "good Anthropocene," there is, e.g., the Breakthrough Institute, thebreakthrough.org.

Mother Nature. The air here is not conceived as a medium – the condition of possibility for life – but as a given object in need of human "care" ("Sorge" in Heidegger's German), repair, reform, protection and ultimately, techno-logical remodeling.

A different form of "explicating" the air, however, would be to work exactly on its elemental nature as a medium of life. Here is where the exper-imental approach of Tomás Saraceno's art is located. Explicating the *mediality* of air means taking an *aesthetic* approach to it. This approach tackles both aspects of the medium air as a medium of sustenance (climate), a medium of transport, and contact (meteors). It does so, however, not so much like traditional post-Kantian aesthetics, as a way of producing, understanding and judging works of art, or by transforming air into an object of art. In the deeply and uncannily experimental era of the Anthropocene, an *aesthetics of air* must mean to actually develop an *aisthesis* of the air. *Aisthetis* is an elemen-tary way of intimately relating to all perceptional dimensions of an object: visual, aural, tactile, and olfactory. An *aisthesis of the air* means exploring it in all its sensory qualities – from its (in)visibility and tactile states (such as temperature, humidity, movement) to its inner dynamics, such as winds, drafts, updraft, density – and maybe even the affective qualities of certain weather conditions. Yet, not as a form of climatological modelling, but as a way of rendering these states and dynamics available to human experience and practice. As experimental *aisthesis* – the full, non-reductionist perception of an atmosphere with all our senses – art creates things, spaces, situations, and environments that convey a sense of their bodily, affective and cognitive presence. By doing so, however, art ideally also allows for new and different forms of *being in the air together*: It creates new forms of positioning bodies in spaces, of relating to one another, and calls for new modes of collaboration and communication. A sense of exploring the presence of spaces, situations, and environments. Saraceno's entire work, his spatial installations, synesthetic environments, sculptural works and the experimental events and actions they create, I believe, make an attempt to explore such an *aisthesis of the air.*

     Eva Horn

So too for the *Aerocene* project. Alluding to the Anthropocene, *Aerocene* gauges the diagnosis of an indelible human impact on the planet by exactly *reversing* its gesture: no impact, no intervention, and no transformation. Nevertheless, it is a form of explicating the air, exploring its structure, its dynamics, its flows, and its density. It might therefore also be about ultimately probing the possibilities of humans "inhabiting the air."[Bronislaw Szerzsynski, *Up*, in *Aerocene* newspaper, Berlin: Studio Tomás Saraceno, 2015: 15.] Yet, unlike classical experiments in the modern age, Saraceno does so without consuming, altering or destroying the object of this investigation. He barely stirs it.

The *Aerocene's* fundamental approach is an exploration of the air from an energetic point of view, both in a climatic and a meteorological way. Most forms of entering the "aerial ocean" rely on heavier-than-air objects, such as airplanes, helicopters or rockets. Even balloons, blimps and the bodies of birds and insects need either fuels, lighter-than-air gases, or muscular strength to stay in the air. They are more (birds, insects, balloons, blimps) or less (airplanes etc.) efficient at exploiting their sources of energy. *Aerocene*, on the contrary, explores the potentialities of lighter-than-air objects that float only powered by the medium itself: by the differential of temperature and density between the air inside and outside the lightweight envelope or sphere of foil. This implies, as Bronislaw Szerszynski has pointed out, a different "metabolic regime."[Ibid.] Directing his projects *upwards,* toward the air and the sun, Saraceno departs from the historical metabolic regimes that either exploit the surface of the Earth (in agriculture) or the fossil fuels stocked below the Earth's crust. Instead, he investigates the possibilities of an energy regime that taps into no resource other than solar radiation and the states and flows of the air.

How long does it take to warm up the air pocket inside an envelope of fabric into buoyancy? How much upward traction can the rays of the sun alone create? How much payload can be lifted under which weather conditions? Where will the flows of the air take it, and when will the air cool down so that the sculpture can land? Working with climatologists and experts on the flow dynamics of the atmosphere, Saraceno's artistic research taps into its very scientific knowledge. By working on the development of sculptures that can go up into the stratosphere, he contributes to this current research. Art becomes science. Yet ultimately, he goes beyond that.

The focus of Saraceno's investigation is the energy of the medium air. The point here is not the overused concept of "zero-energy" that helps sell solar panels, house insulation and wind parks. Saraceno's works, on the contrary, are full of energy in every respect. There is energy stored in materials, their elasticity, durability, and inner tensions; energy in the form of the stability or dynamics of certain geometrical forms; last but not least, *social energy* in the new modes of participation, collaboration and community, forming the basis of most of the *Aerocene* activities, as well as the travelling *Museo Aero Solar.*

Thus, the point is not zero-energy but *zero-metabolism.* This means refraining from the use of any kind of fuel, gas, or physical energy. The gist is to utilize the medium air, without using it up.

Here is where I see Saraceno's departure from a merely scientific approach to the air. Much like the old forms of knowledge, he thinks about air as a *social medium,* and about an ethical and political attitude toward that medium. What can we do with things, with environments, with atmospheres – and maybe also with human beings – without, in one way or another, consuming them, burning them up in our industrial, economic, social, or even emotional metabolisms? Saraceno's attitude seems to be one of preservation, a grasp on things that is essentially non-consumptive, non-appropriative but rather passive, resourceful, intelligently frugal, and sharing.

The general idea here is to exploit the material properties of an object without wasting it. To re-use, re-purpose, maybe even to "hack" objects into new forms of functionality. This, as opposed to recycling, which just feeds the object into a new (often highly energy-intensive) metabolic cycle. Hence the idea of re-using the obnoxious and omnipresent plastic shopping bags that pollute cities, landscapes and oceans. In the various stations of *Museo Aero Solar,* in Vienna, Milan, Toulouse and other places around the globe, the community of enthusiasts and locals re-purposed them by building vast, airy spaces. The incidental, yet intense and cheerful form of do-it-together that the *Museo Aero Solar* calls for and creates, refrains from feeding into the usual

Museo Aero Solar is a flying museum, a solar balloon completely made up of reused plastic bags, with new sections being added each time it travels the world, thus changing techniques, drawings and shapes, and growing in size every time it sets sail in the air. Museo Aero Solar stands for a different conception of space and energy both anomalous and forceful at the same time. The core of the Museo resides in the inventiveness of local inhabitants, not in its image: among collective action and art, do-it-together technology and experimentation, it is a voyage back/forward in time. Alberto Pesavento and Tomás Saraceno initiated it in Milan, 2007. www.museoaerosolar.wordpress.com.

modes of participation, such as production, service or exchange. A spontaneous and voluntary gathering and a playful, non-commercial experiment: to make something float in the sky with just the power of the air. The mediality of air incorporates you into a community, using simple tools such as glue and scissors, warming the air inside with the warmth of moving, chatting, laughing bodies.

Being in the air, as the Ancient authors knew, has not just a physical, but also a social and affective dimension. It is about the social atmosphere that people create with each other, the way they conjointly "inhabit the air," cooperate in forming and transforming it, and the way they move and travel in it. Spheres, the fundamental element of many Saraceno installations, are about the possibility of creating social communities by creating microclimates through insulation. Spheres create an artificial climate insulated from the climate at large, they allow for warmer or colder spaces than the outside world. "Insulation," the building of insulated spheres, is thus a primary element of civilization, be it through clothing or housing. Many of the *Aerocene* experiments work with such closed spheres, e.g. the installation at Grand Palais during the COP21 Conference in Paris – reflecting models of the gigantic, yet existentially closed and finite sphere we inhabit, as well as the many insulated smaller sub-spheres we create inside of it. The *Aerocene* installation is a plurality of spheres commenting on the unity of the Earth's atmosphere. As Bruno Latour states, "spheres are … complex ecosystems in which forms of life define their "immunity" by devising protective walls and inventing elaborate systems of air conditioning. Inside those artificial spheres of existence, humans are born and raised."[Bruno Latour, "Some Experiments in Art and Politics," *E-Flux Journal*, 23, March 2011, www.e-flux.com/journal/23/67790/some-experiments-in-art-and-politics.] While these spheres may explore and comment on the climatic side of air and our dwelling there, Saraceno's recent projects within *Aerocene* seem to focus more on the meteorological side of air, our moving in and with it. In the various flights staged in Poland and Germany, Cappadocia, Salar de Uyuni in Bolivia, and White Sands dunes in New Mexico, the focus is not the closedness and climatic insulation in the sphere, but the energy and dynamics of the air.

In the model of the trajectory of one sculpture from its starting point east of Berlin to its landing in Poland, we get a sense of what Saraceno is after: a new form of translocating in and inhabiting the air that he likes to refer to as *Cloud Cities*. The camera, lifting up, records a gaze that tracks the movement and journey of the hovering vehicle. A travelling shot of the meteorological currents and drifts within the atmosphere. This gaze anticipates lightweight human travel on these winds, being carried away at random and nomadically – or rather aimlessly following the infinitely complex pattern of airflows, updrafts and downdrafts. This exploration of the meteorological side of air, its dynamics, fluxes and different energetic states, opens up a utopian possibility for humans to move within and through these flows. Our way of travelling today is purposeful, technologically controlled, and energetically wasteful: a projection of bodies from A to B in a heavier-than-air vehicle. As opposed to the signature mode of displacement in the Anthropocene, the airplane trip, *Aerocene* travel would enable bodies to enter the gigantic conveyor belts of the winds, the mere energy of the atmosphere. Lifted up by the sculpture, one could travel at random, open to lands where the wind takes the vehicle. The trajectory of the floating sculpture opens up a time and space that relinquishes the iron grip of human purpose and control to the soft whims of the air. Softly lifting by daylight and gently sinking by night. Delicately reflecting the landscapes below, and being reflected by them.

Here, I believe, lies the gentle utopian vision of Saraceno's uplifting endeavors; to be open to the randomness of the winds, to passively abandon ourselves to the flows that make life possible. Not to control and not to consume. In an *Aerocene* future, humankind would float around the globe like Humboldt's seeds, dust, and pollen. Life floating within its own medium.

   Eva Horn

Notes on Aerocene

by Tomás Saraceno

This is my favorite place on Earth,

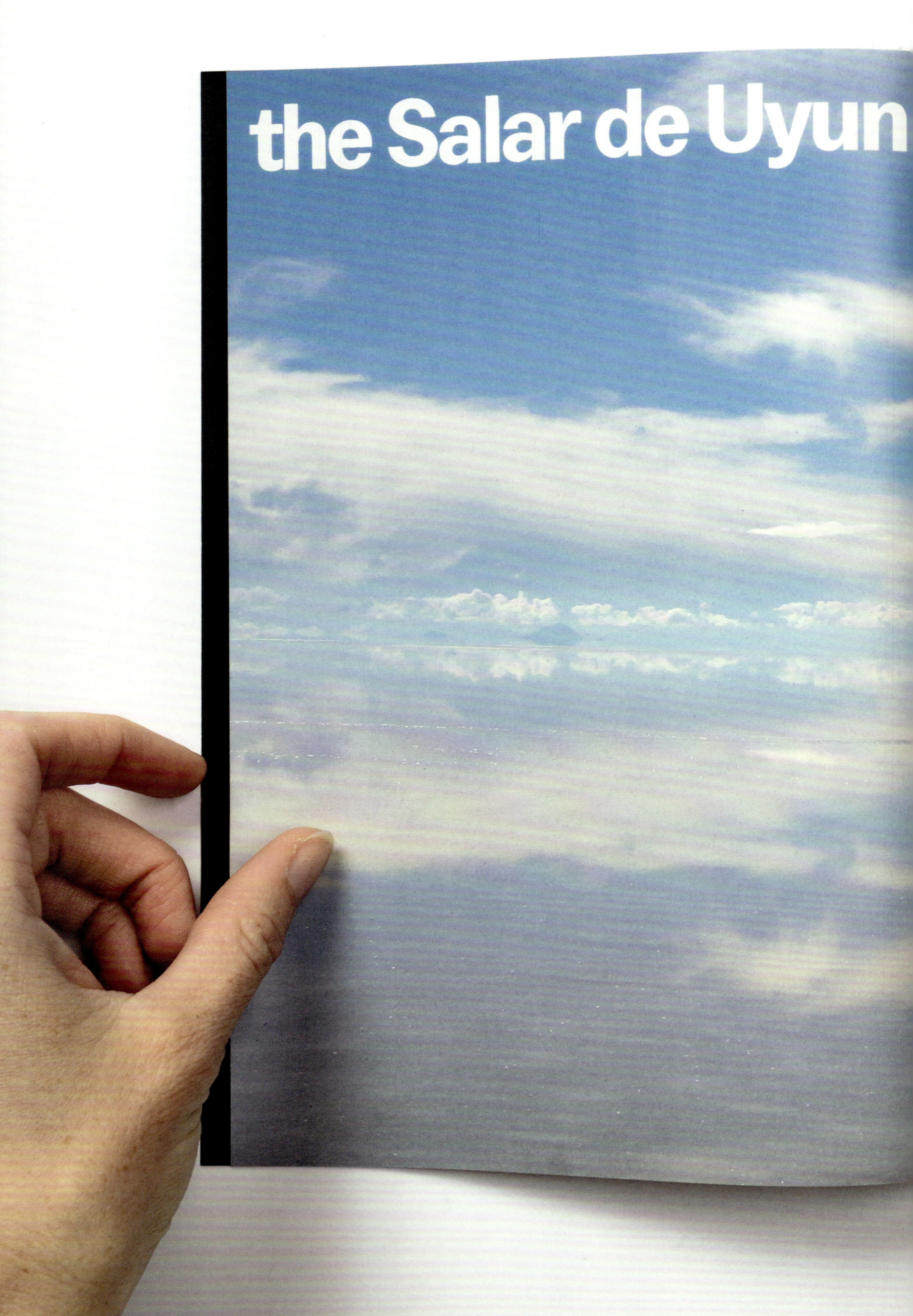

the Salar de Uyun

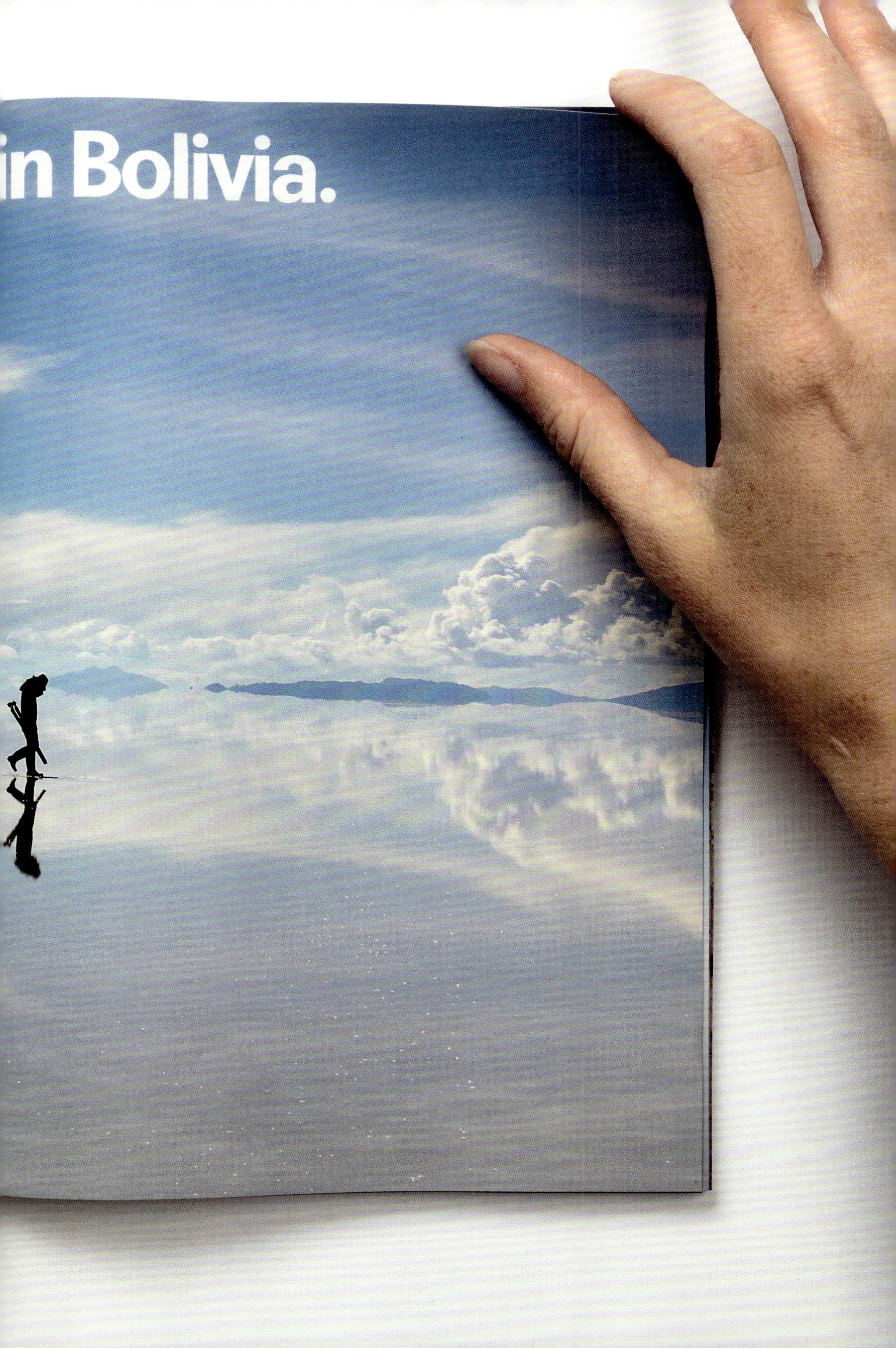
in Bolivia.

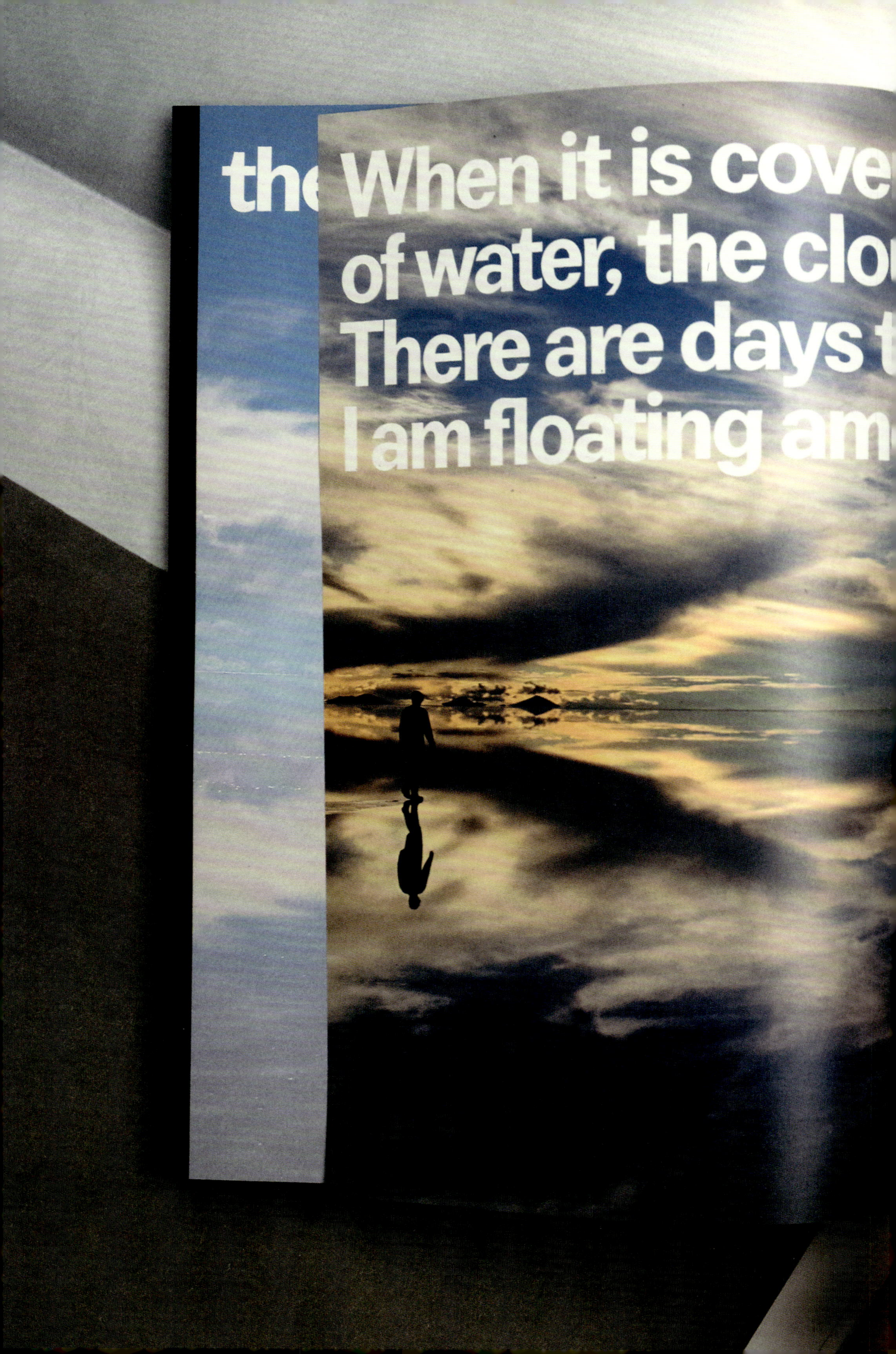

the When it is cove
of water, the clo
There are days t
I am floating am

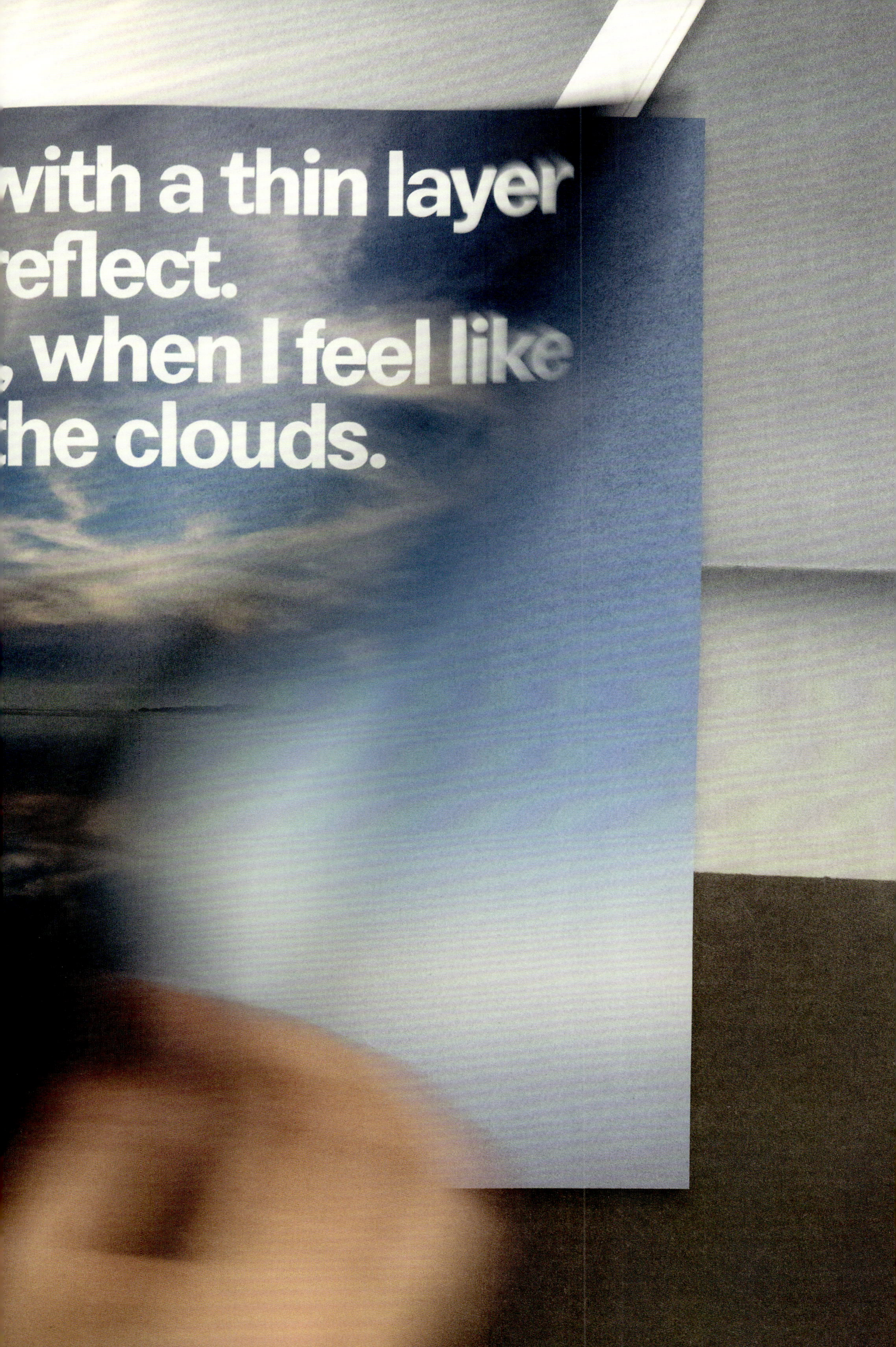
with a thin layer
reflect.
when I feel like
the clouds.

When the horizo
there is no abov

disappears,
nor below.

One night I awoke i
of a dream, and sav
in the water.

the middle
stars reflected

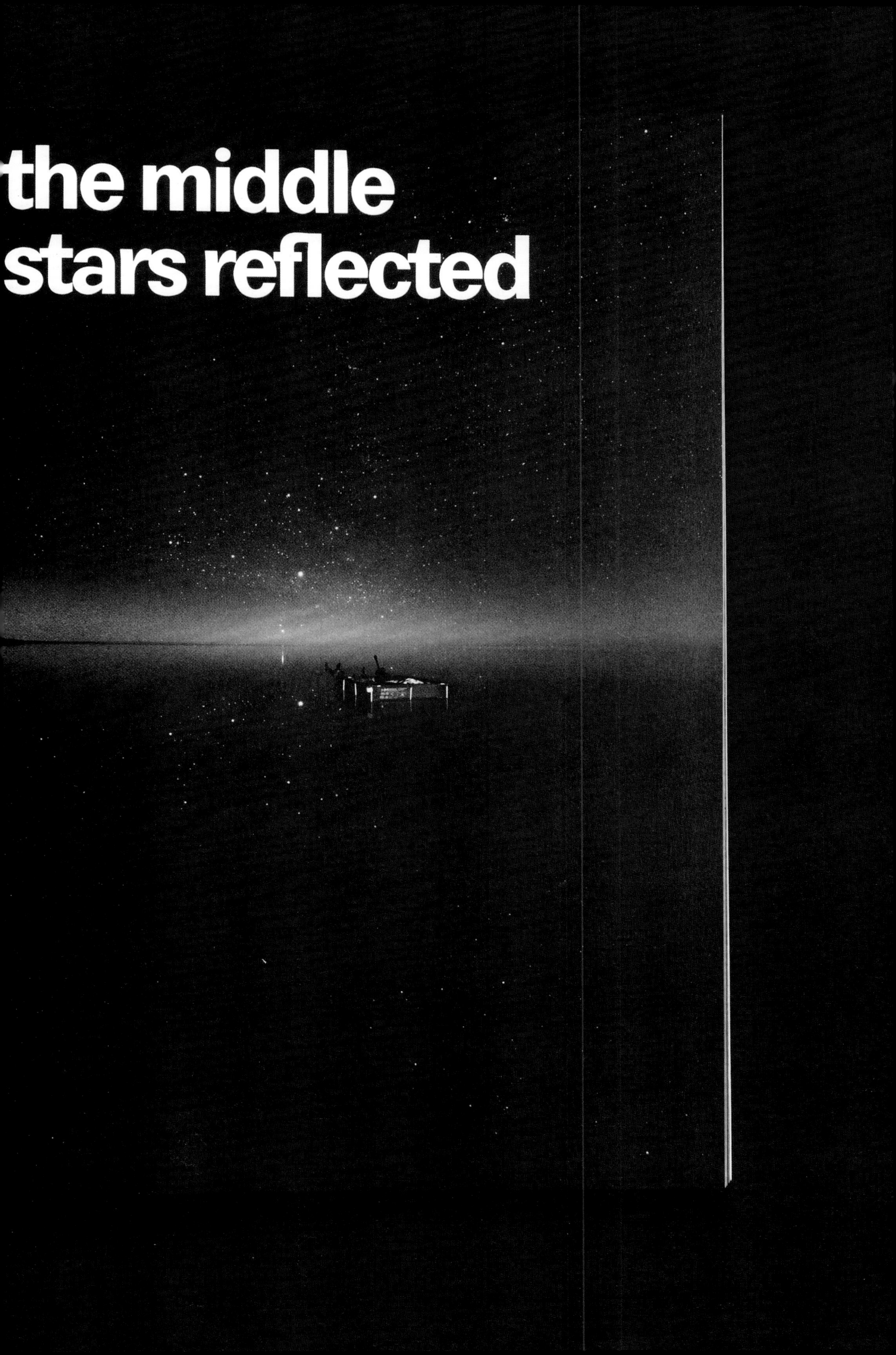

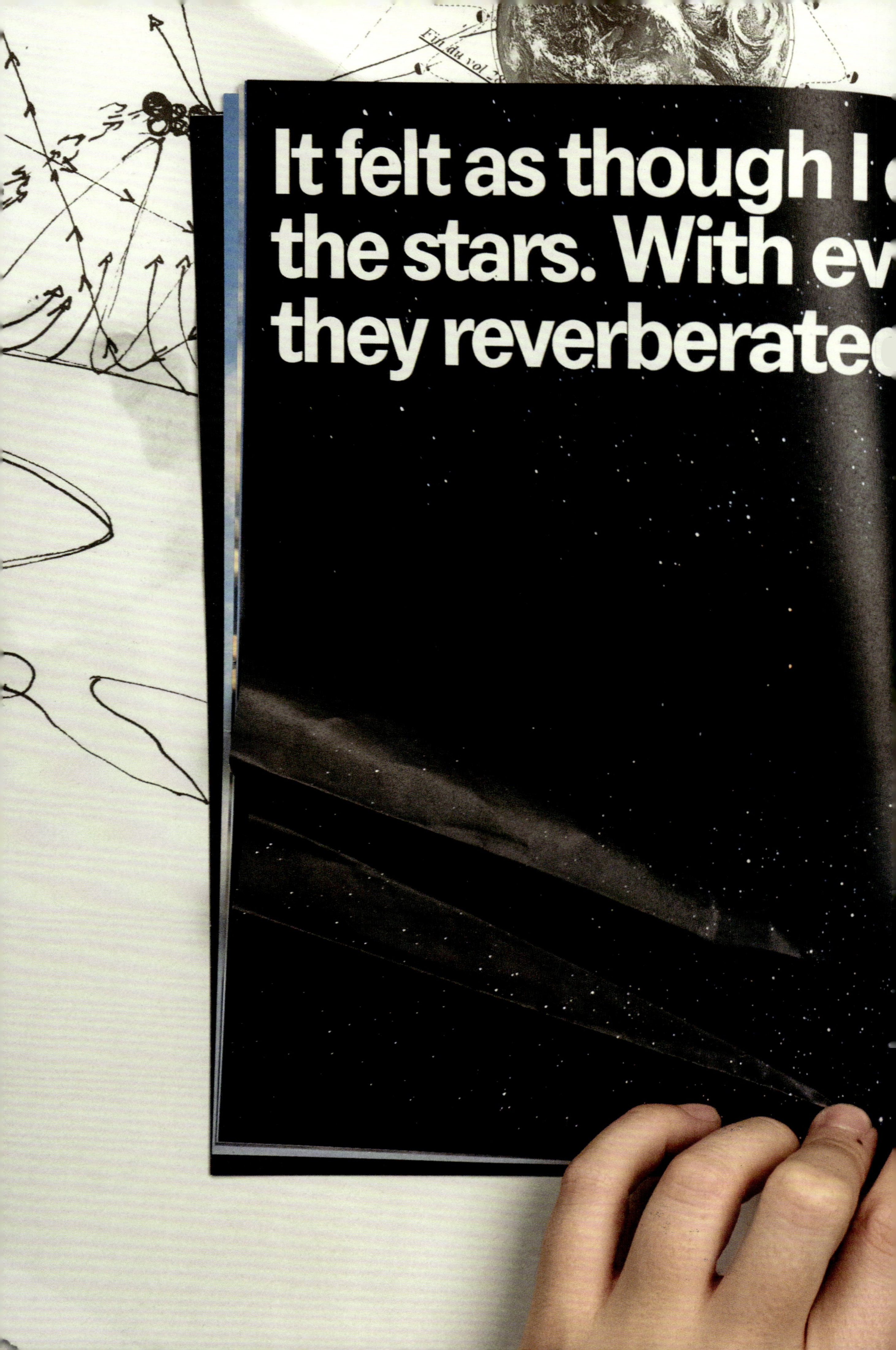
It felt as though I
the stars. With ev
they reverberated

ld walk among

step I took,

It was like
floating in t
among clouds c

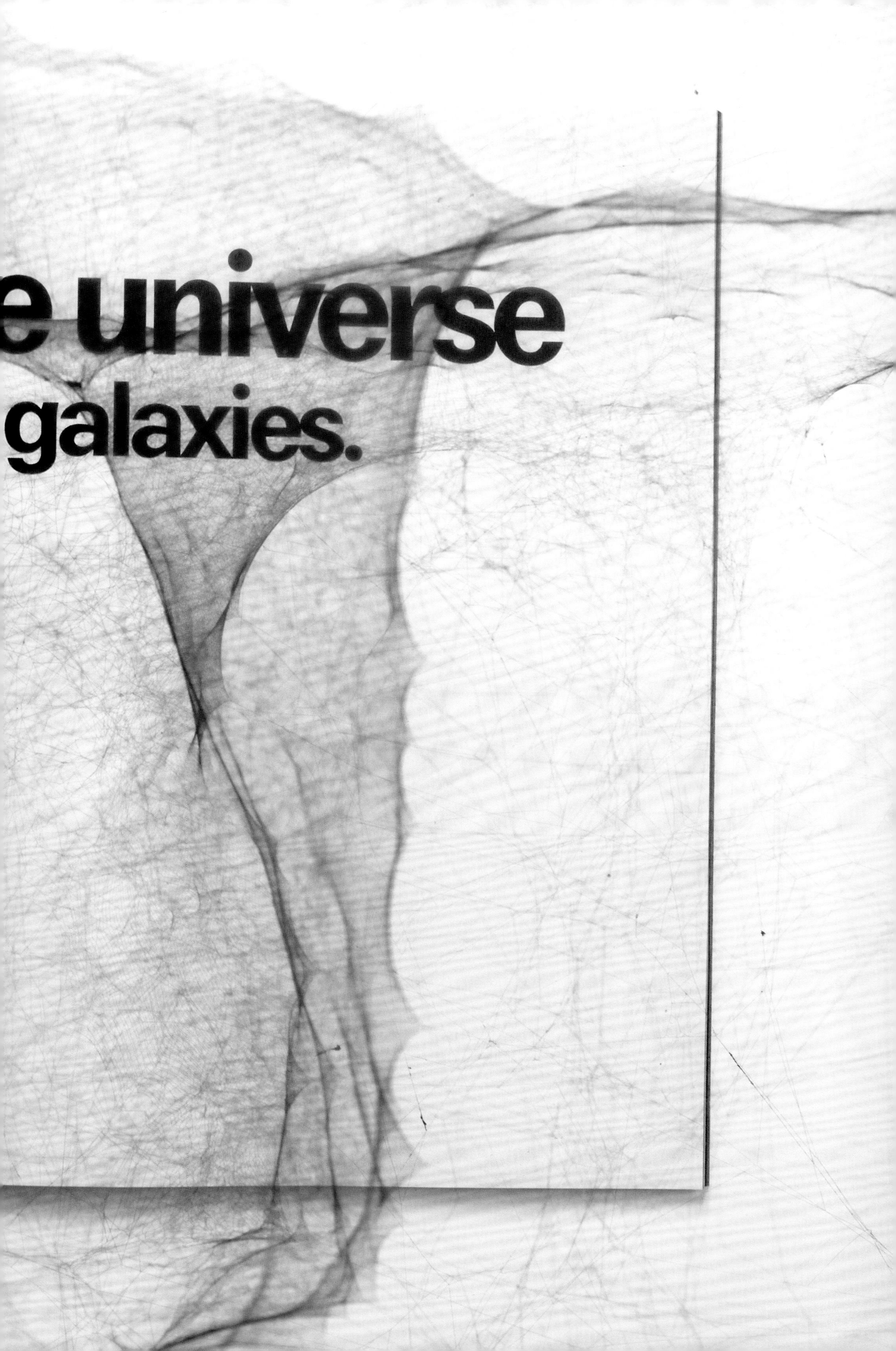
e universe
galaxies.

But the reality is
what floats in the water
today are not clouds
of galaxies, but clouds
of plastic.

When we look up,
we are confronted
by traces of pollution,
of toxicity forming
clouds that pollute
our dreams.

These traces on
the marks of a pr
new epoch, leavi
on terrestrial eco

This time has be
Anthropo

e planet are
posed
g a global impact
ystems.

named the

cene.

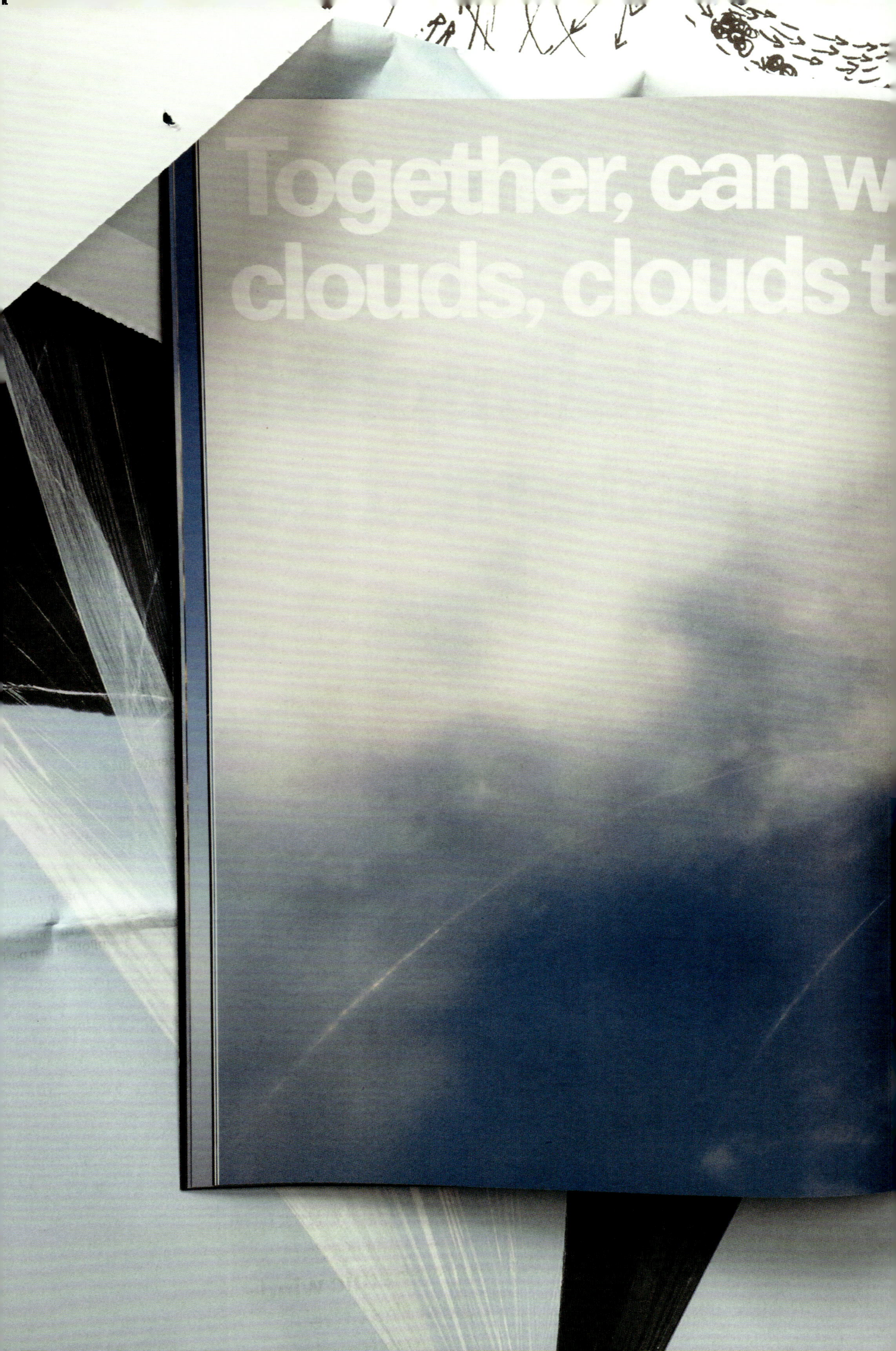
Together, can w
clouds, clouds t

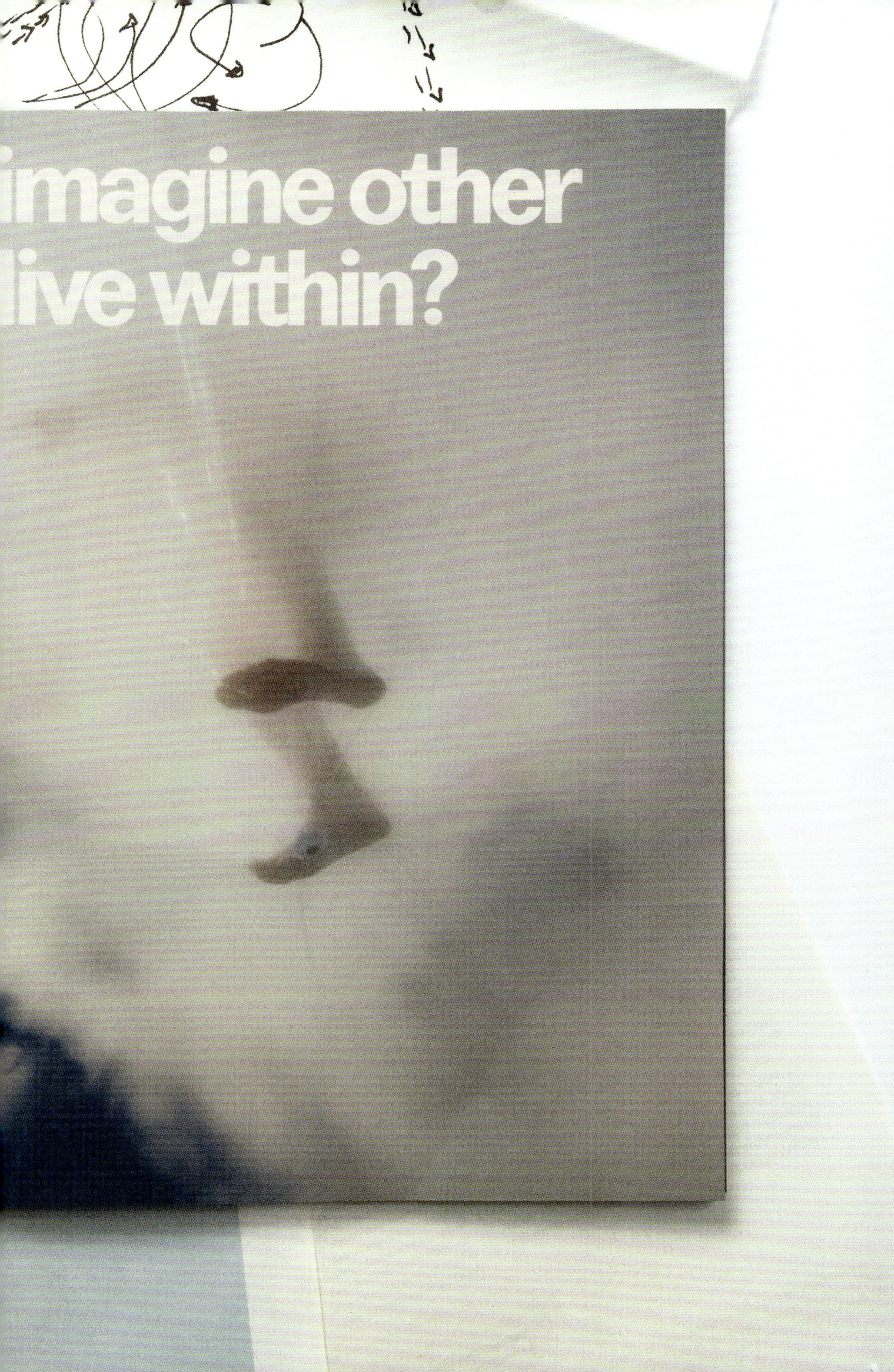
imagine other
live within?

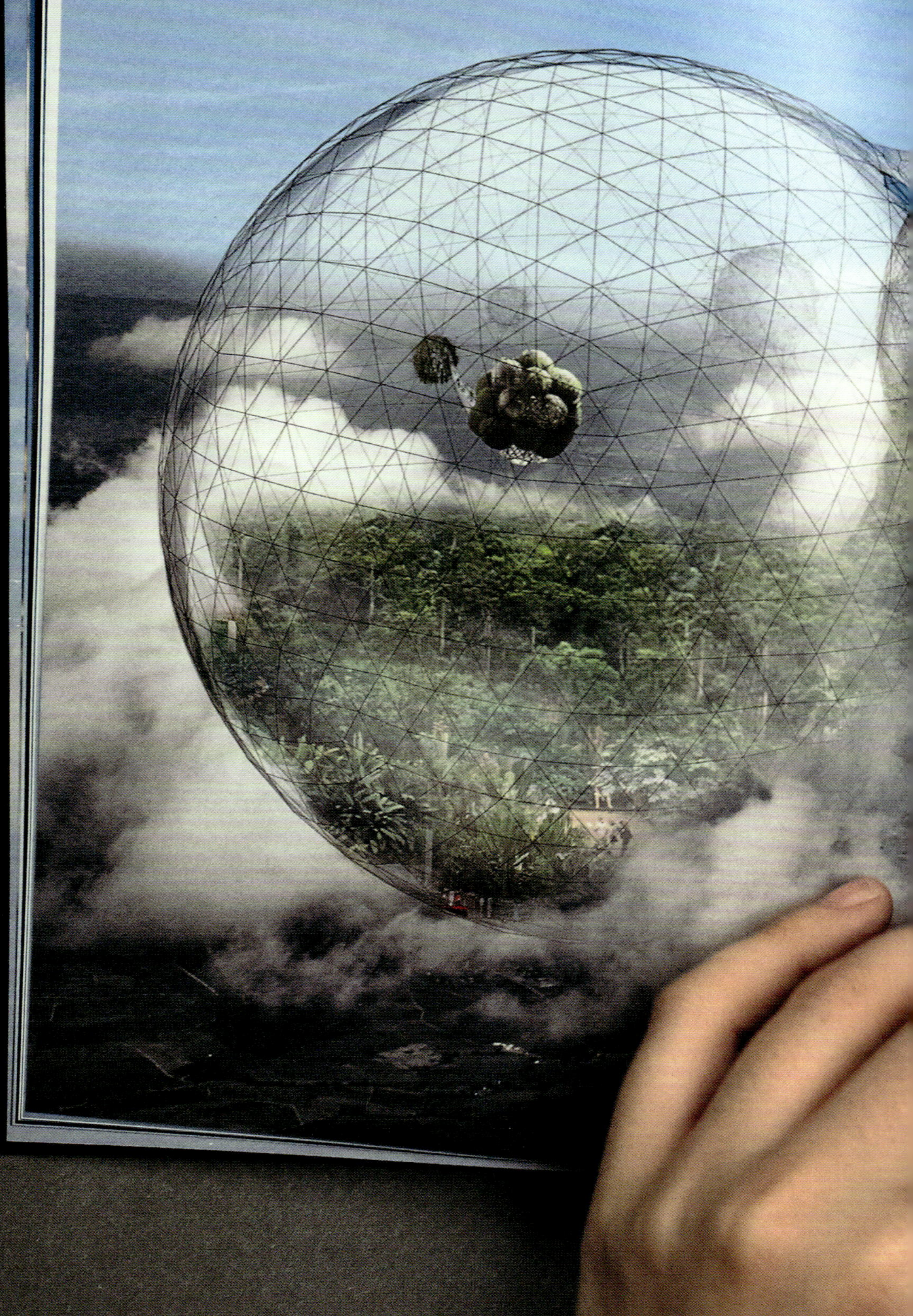

How can we floa

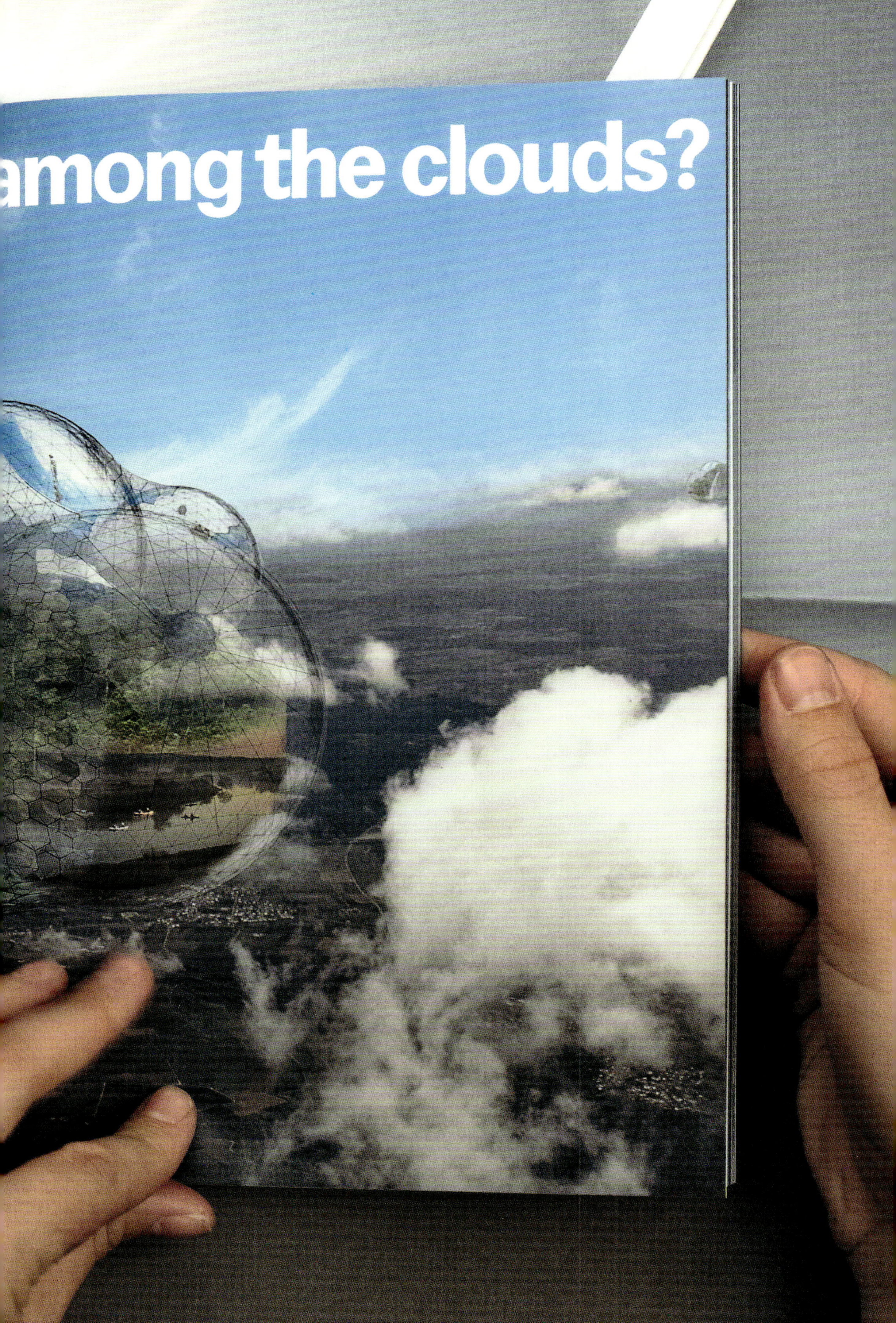
among the clouds?

s into creative dialogue with multiple departments
oss the Institute. Moving among practical, theo-
cal and hypothetical considerations, Saraceno
ussed everything from nanoengineered materials
lar energy to weather patterns to the origins of
niverse, asking architects, engineer
n diverse fields to imagine w
reality might look like. A w
isparate areas of expertise
p a productive collaboratio
climatologist whose specia
heric dynamics, and Bill M
ctural training led him to he
heric and Planetary Sciences
ations of geophysical fluid dyn
n "to make people understa
" (her words), they began wi
a series of rotating fluid lab
eated by Illari and Professor

e is the latest node in Tomás S
experimentation with solar b
is own do-it-yourself versions
r by sun power, 2003), crowd-
de with plastic shopping bags
ing since 2007), and a resider
ationale d'Études Spatiales)
studying their MIR (*Montgo*
balloon flights. Now Illari and
e MIR flight data to visualize
new series of solar balloons
hemical components of the st
their effect on climate change.
a gathering scientific data i
g with his capacity to work at
of expression and registers o
o also sees these balloons as
ures" and as an opportunity for
twork of participants to monit
ict the weather collectively, a
r technological disruptions of
narios outlined below link te
onary thinking and material r
tream art research center" – "
king.

m the past
nfraRouge (MIR)
o has focused upon infrared/
gy which he has dubbed aeros
o energy consumption that ca
om the sun during the day
during the night. This technol
d by CNES (the Centre Natio
in the 1970s, can be used as
no believes, for how mankir
symbiosis with the earth, spar
n and inspiring the public t
ation at a time when the earth
ulation and climate change.
on is 'zero-energy' and yet ca
obe much like the albatross o
ut flying much higher, even up
One could imagine using such
e ozone and other chemicals
stratosphere with nearly zero

h Saraceno, Illari's group at
ata from past balloon flights
nd begun planning future
hat are being developed with

been supporting a program
c flights using hot air bal-
InfraRouge). The MIR is a
which is heated by solar
nfrared radiation from th

ght these multifaceted inter-

nium gas. After 2 or 3 days, the helium is completely
evacuated and the MIR then flies only using hot air –
see Fig. 1 (right).

The MIR balloons have been used to perform
tropical and trans-polar stratospheric flights. As an
example we describe a flight in 200
loon travelled

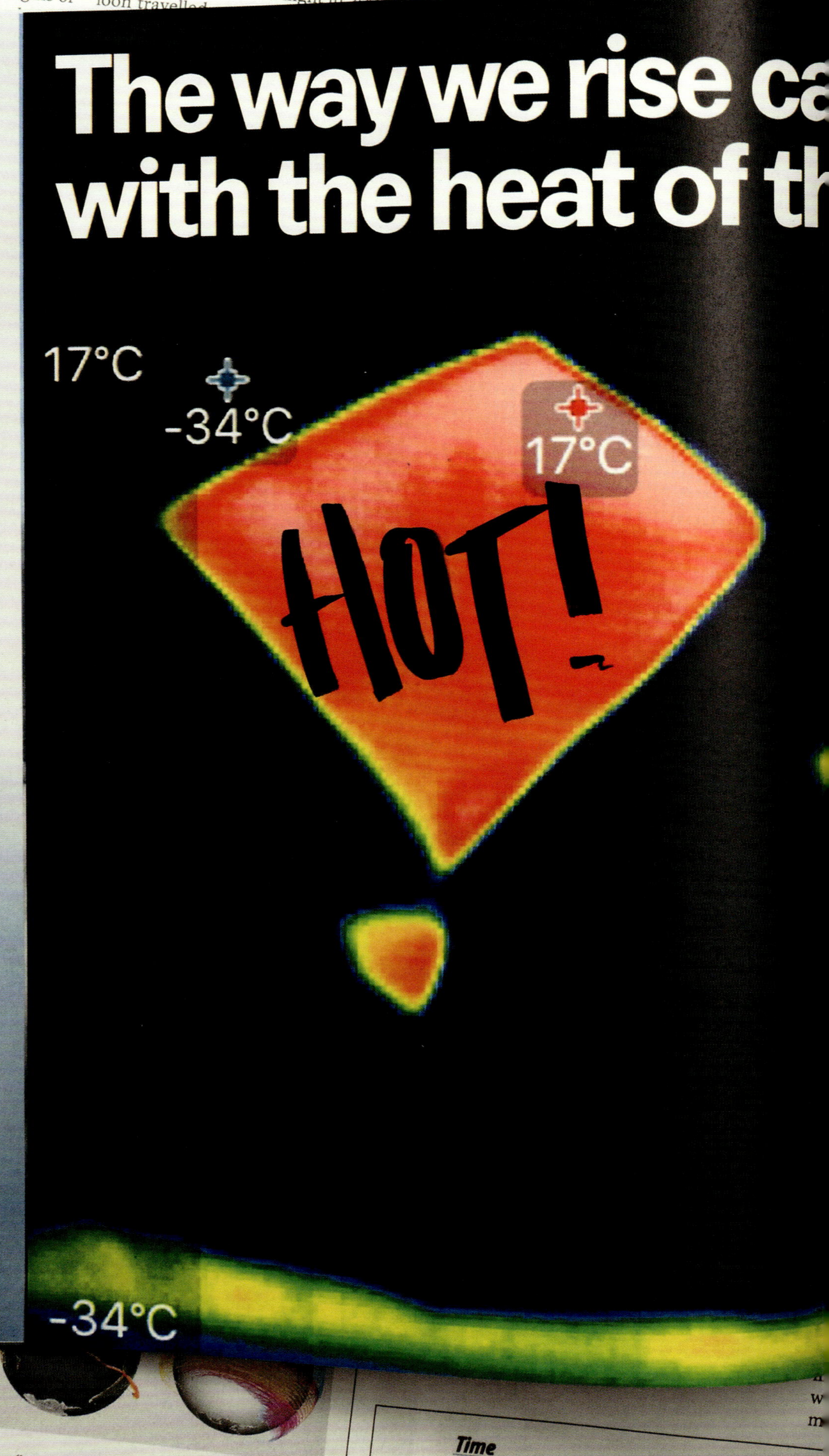

The way we rise ca
with the heat of th

Fig. 3 (left) Observed path of the balloon from February
4th to 14th 2004, as it flies from Brazil to Australia –
daytime is marked orange, nighttime is marked violet.
(right) 30 mb trajectories in February 2004 (10 days travel)
at the same time as the MIR flight. Trajectories color with
the direction of the wind: blue f

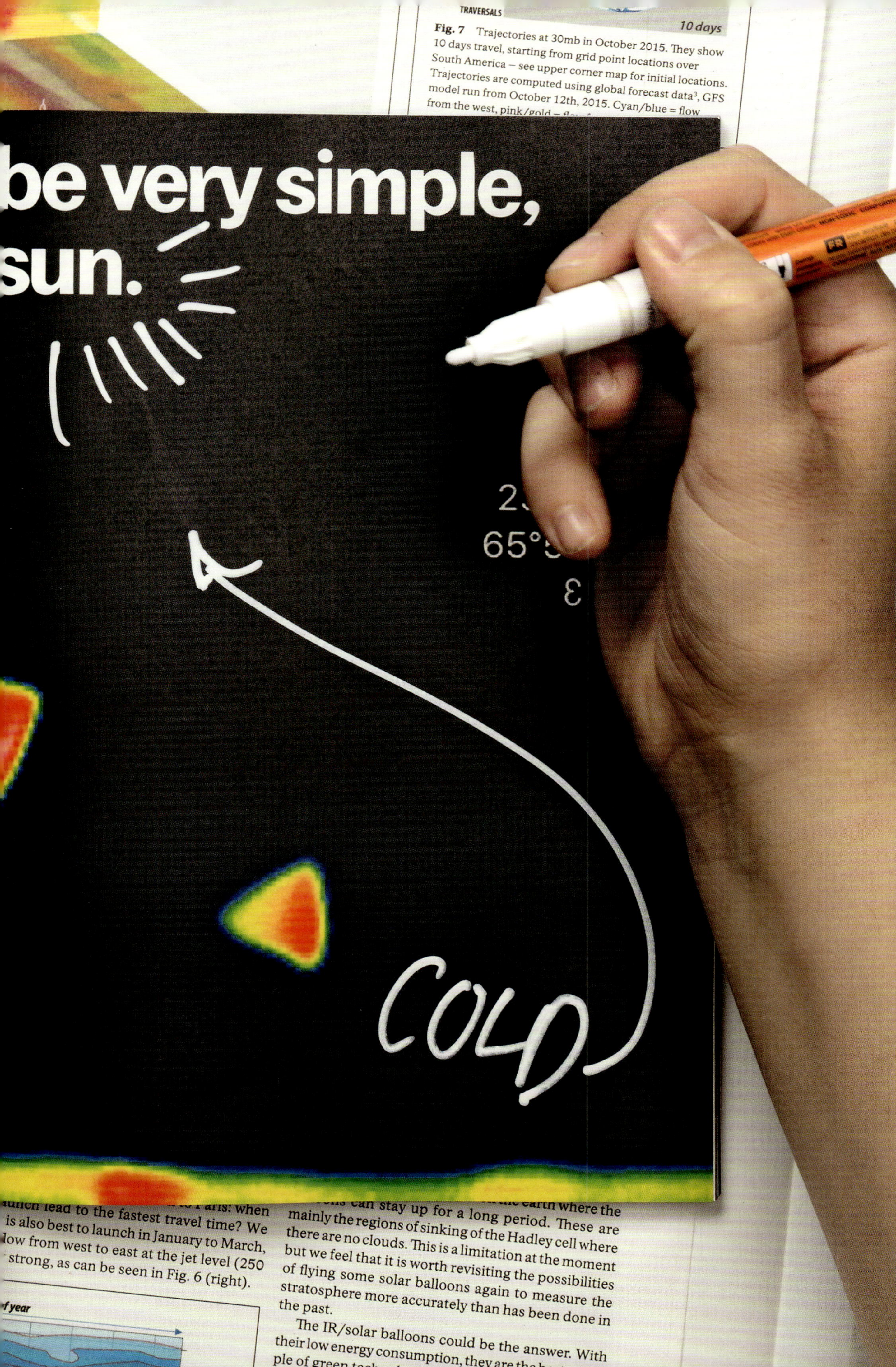
TRAVERSALS
10 days
Fig. 7   Trajectories at 30mb in October 2015. They show
10 days travel, starting from grid point locations over
South America — see upper corner map for initial locations.
Trajectories are computed using global forecast data³, GFS
model run from October 12th, 2015. Cyan/blue = flow
from the west, pink/gold = flow
be very simple,
sun.
COLD
launch lead to the fastest travel time? We
is also best to launch in January to March,
low from west to east at the jet level (250
strong, as can be seen in Fig. 6 (right).
of year
ns can stay up for a long period. These are
mainly the regions of sinking of the Hadley cell where
there are no clouds. This is a limitation at the moment
but we feel that it is worth revisiting the possibilities
of flying some solar balloons again to measure the
stratosphere more accurately than has been done in
the past.
The IR/solar balloons could be the answer. With
their low energy consumption, they are the best
ple of green technol

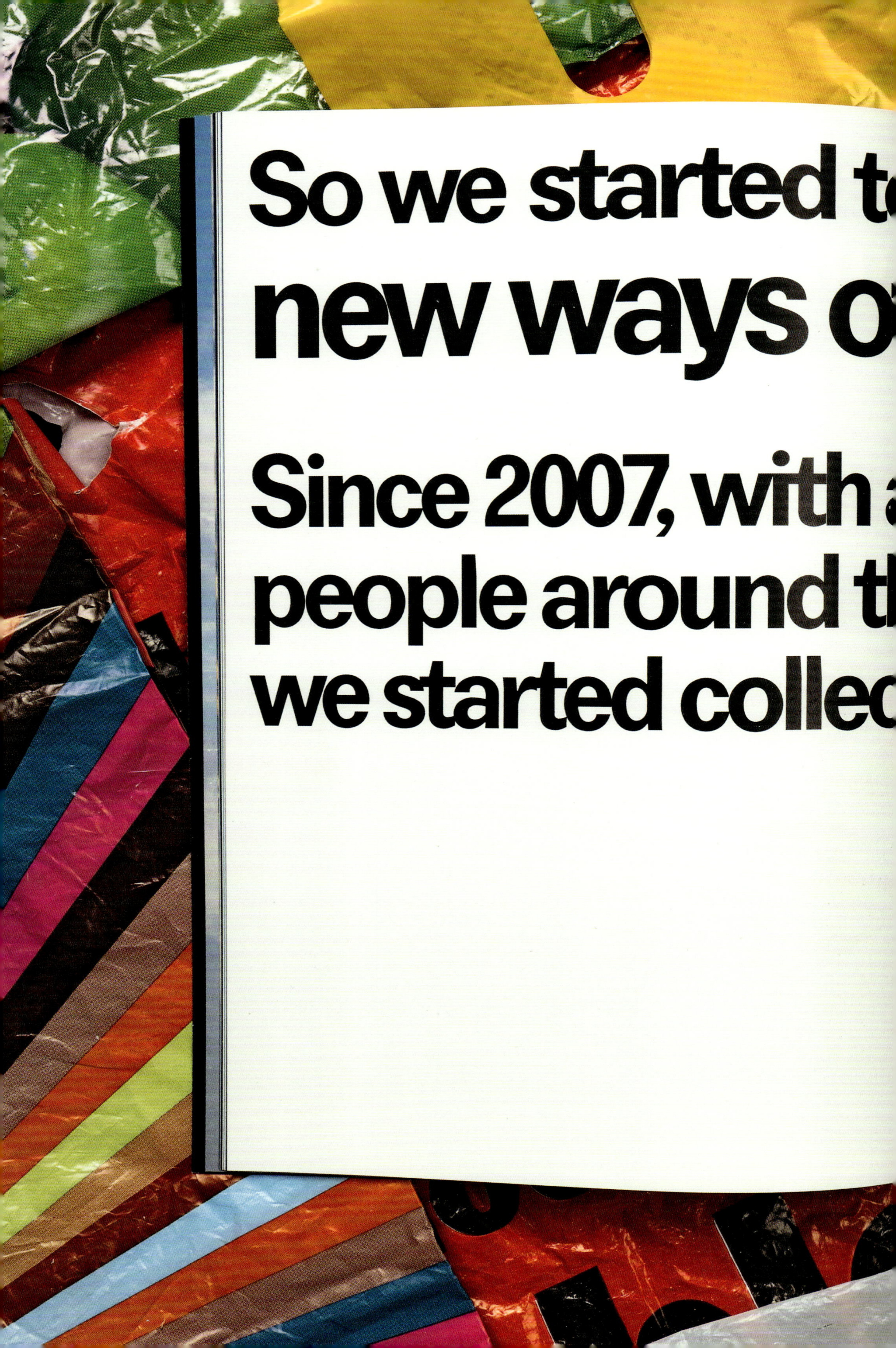
So we started t
new ways o
Since 2007, with a
people around th
we started collec

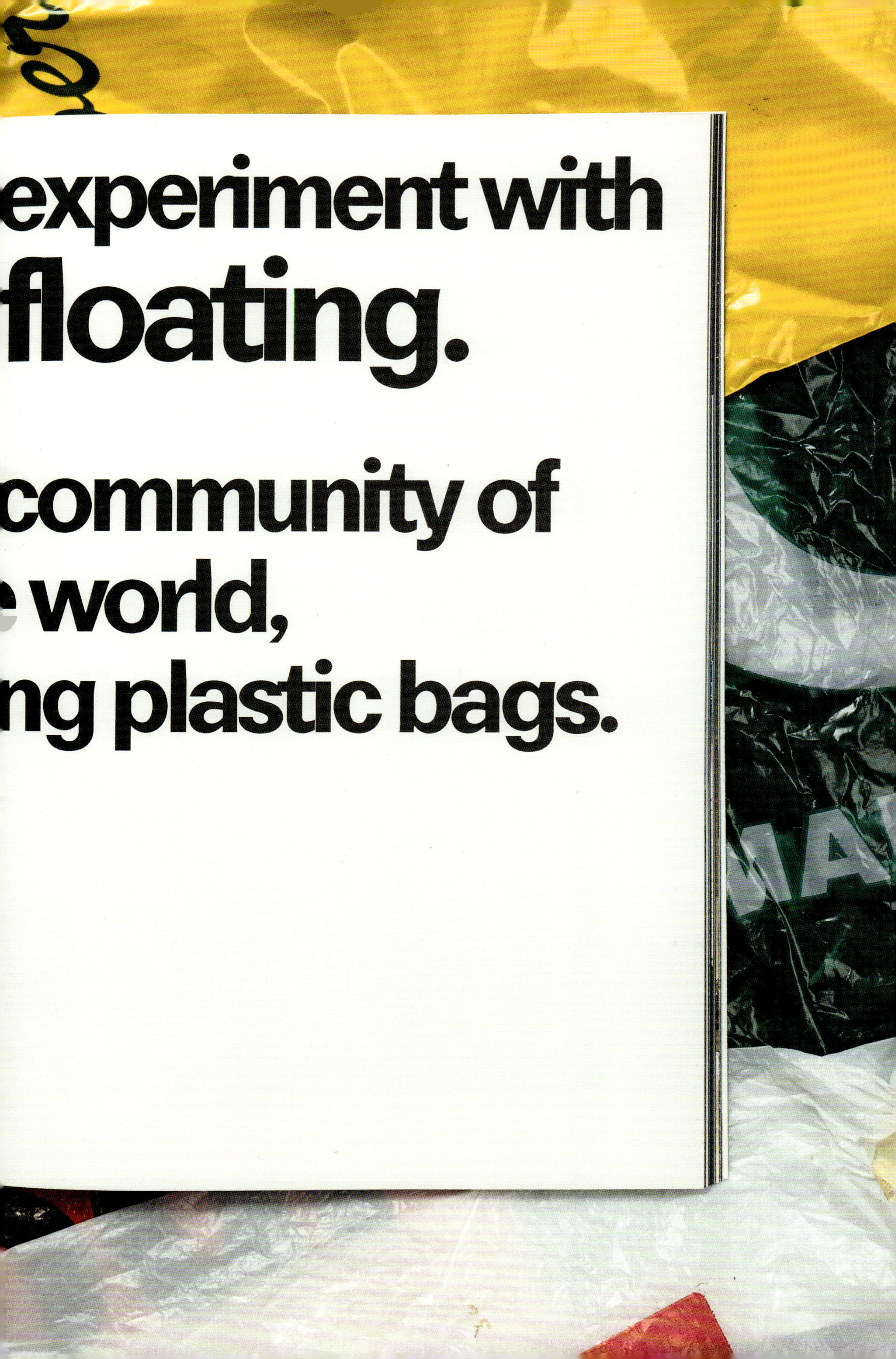
experiment with
floating.

community of
world,
plastic bags.

We wash them.
We dry them.
We take care of them.
We cut them.
We paste them.

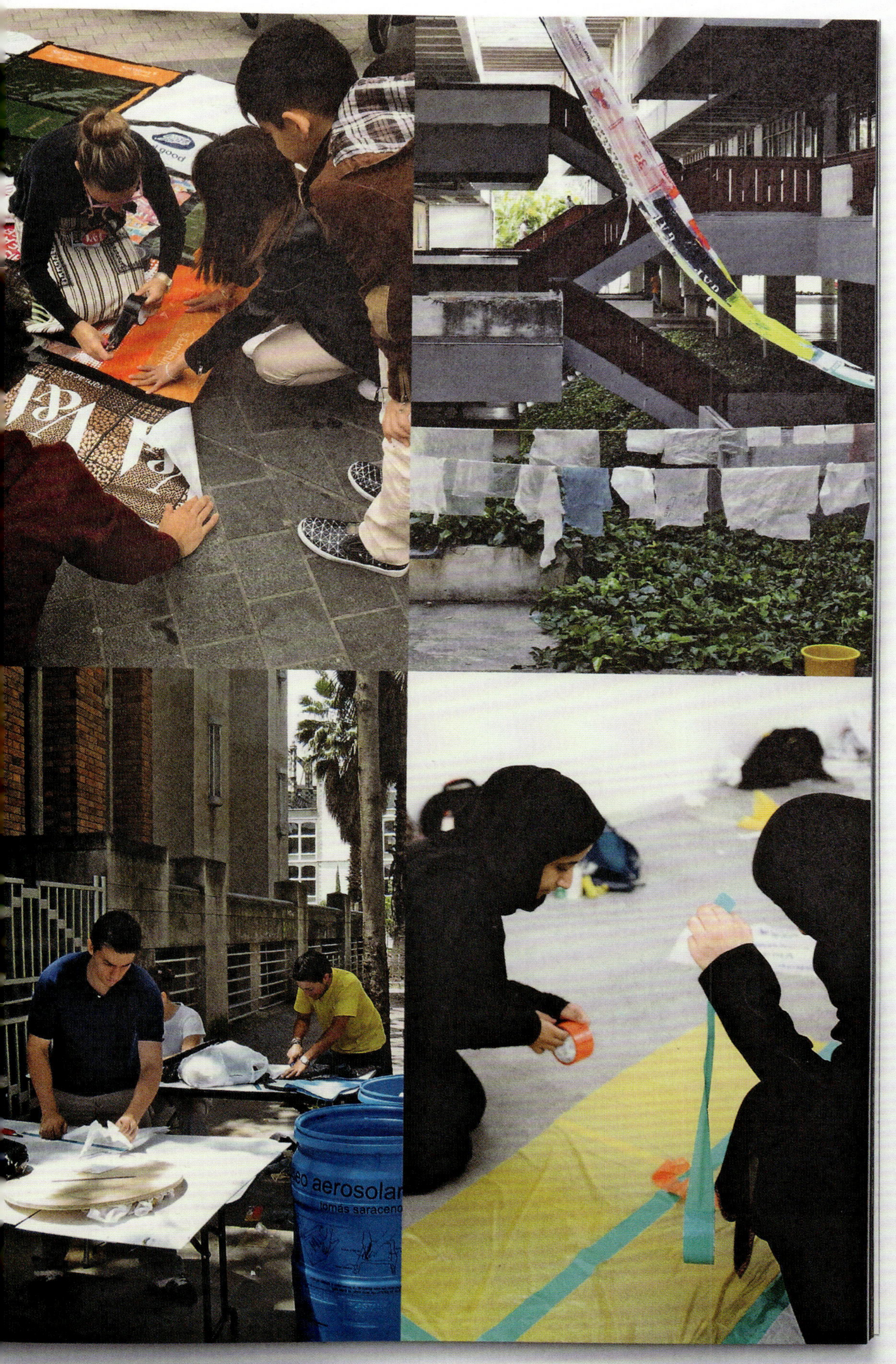

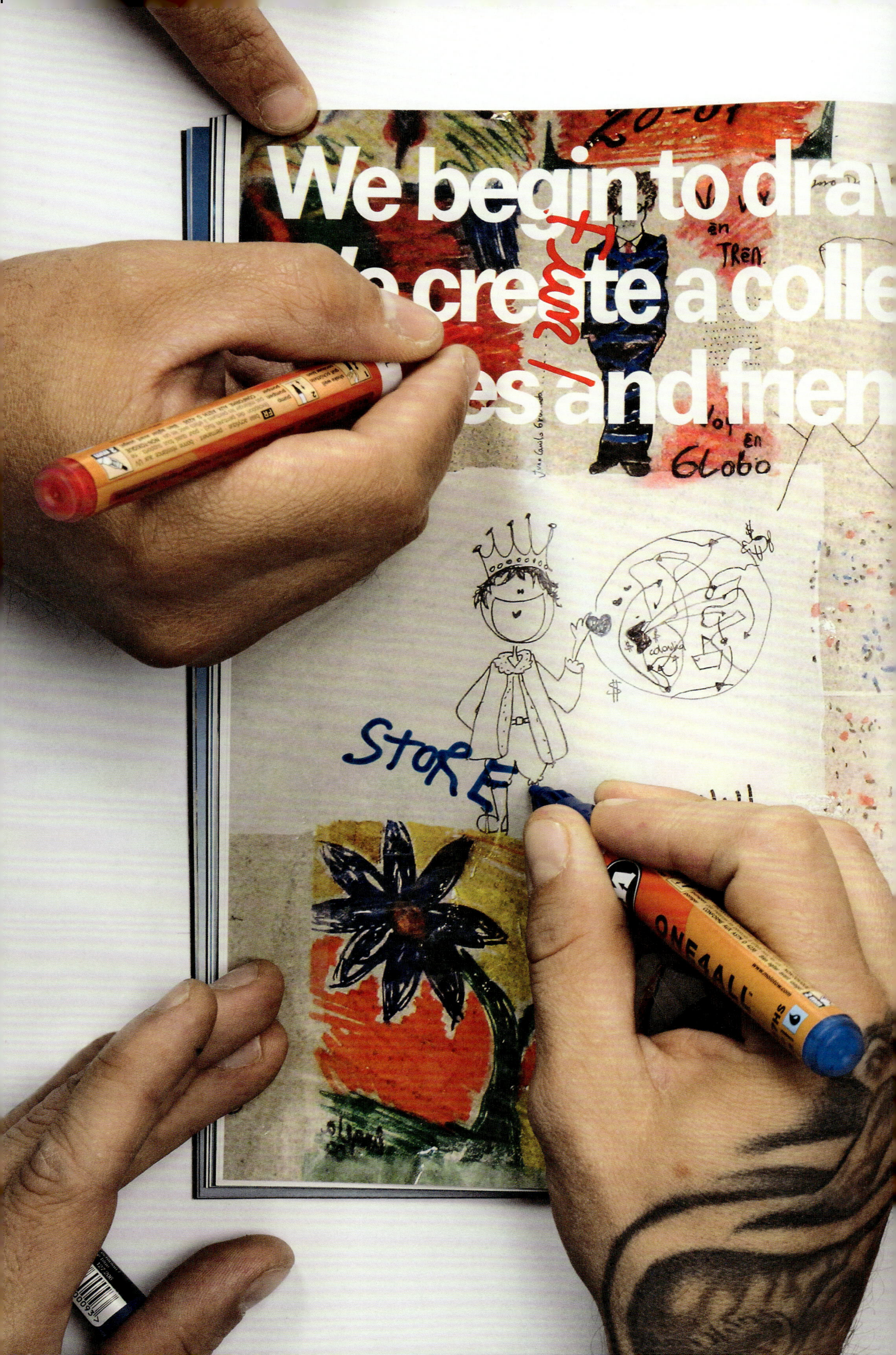

We begin to dra
create a colle
and frien
Fun
STORE

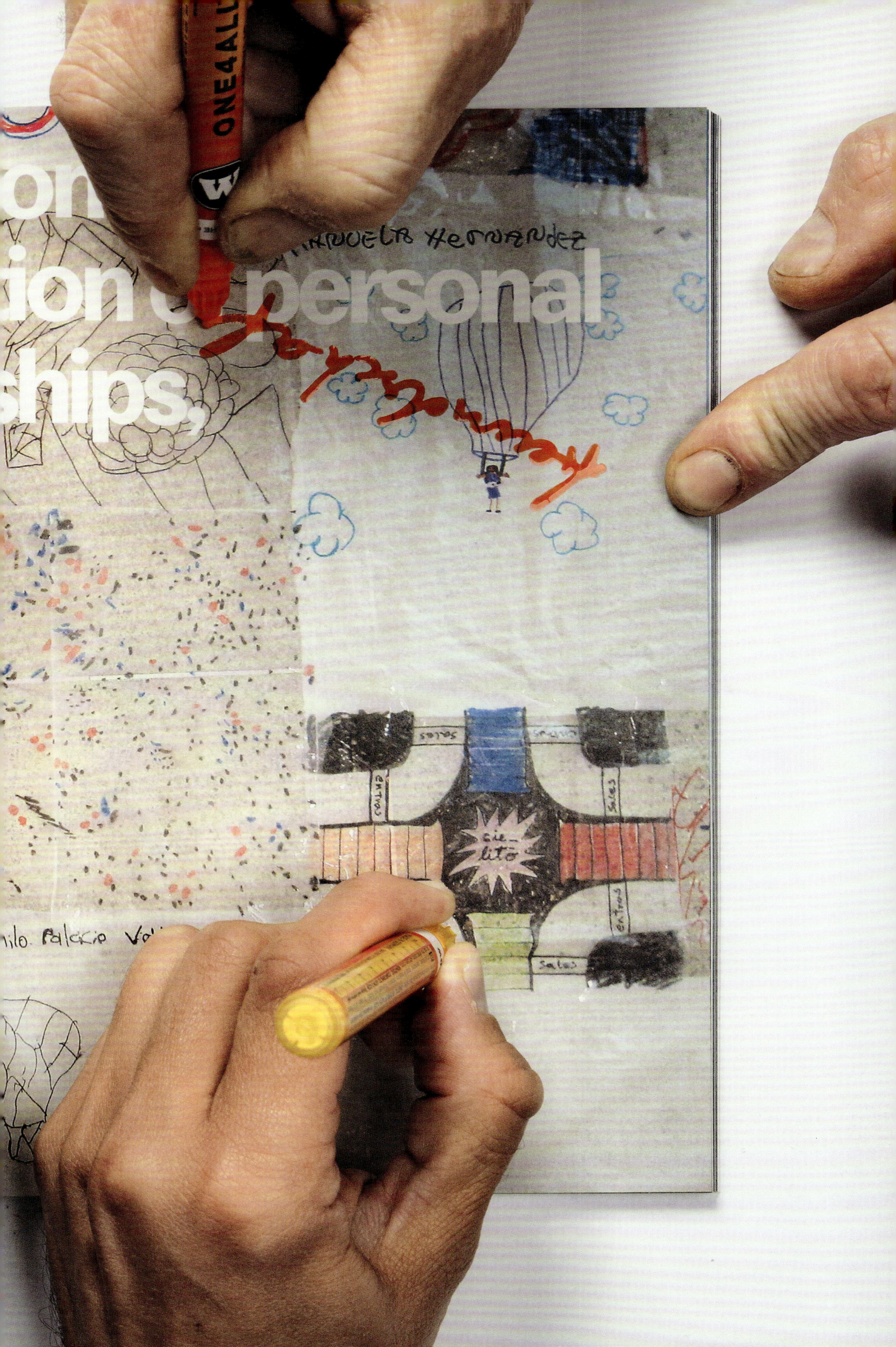

ONE4ALL
ion
ion
ships,
personal
MANUELA HERNANDEZ
ilo Palacio Vo
sie-
lito
sales
centro
sales
salas
salas

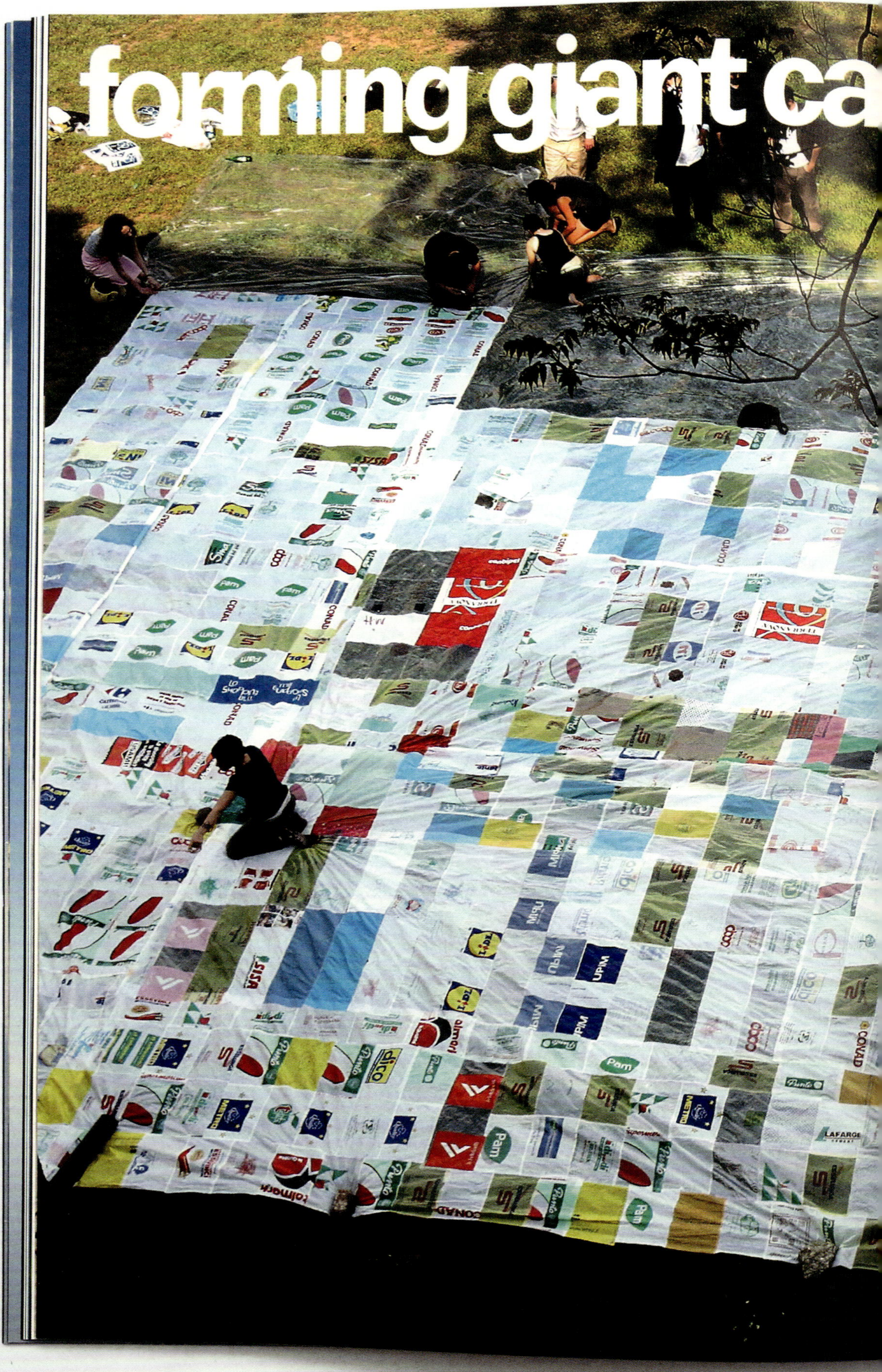
forming giant ca

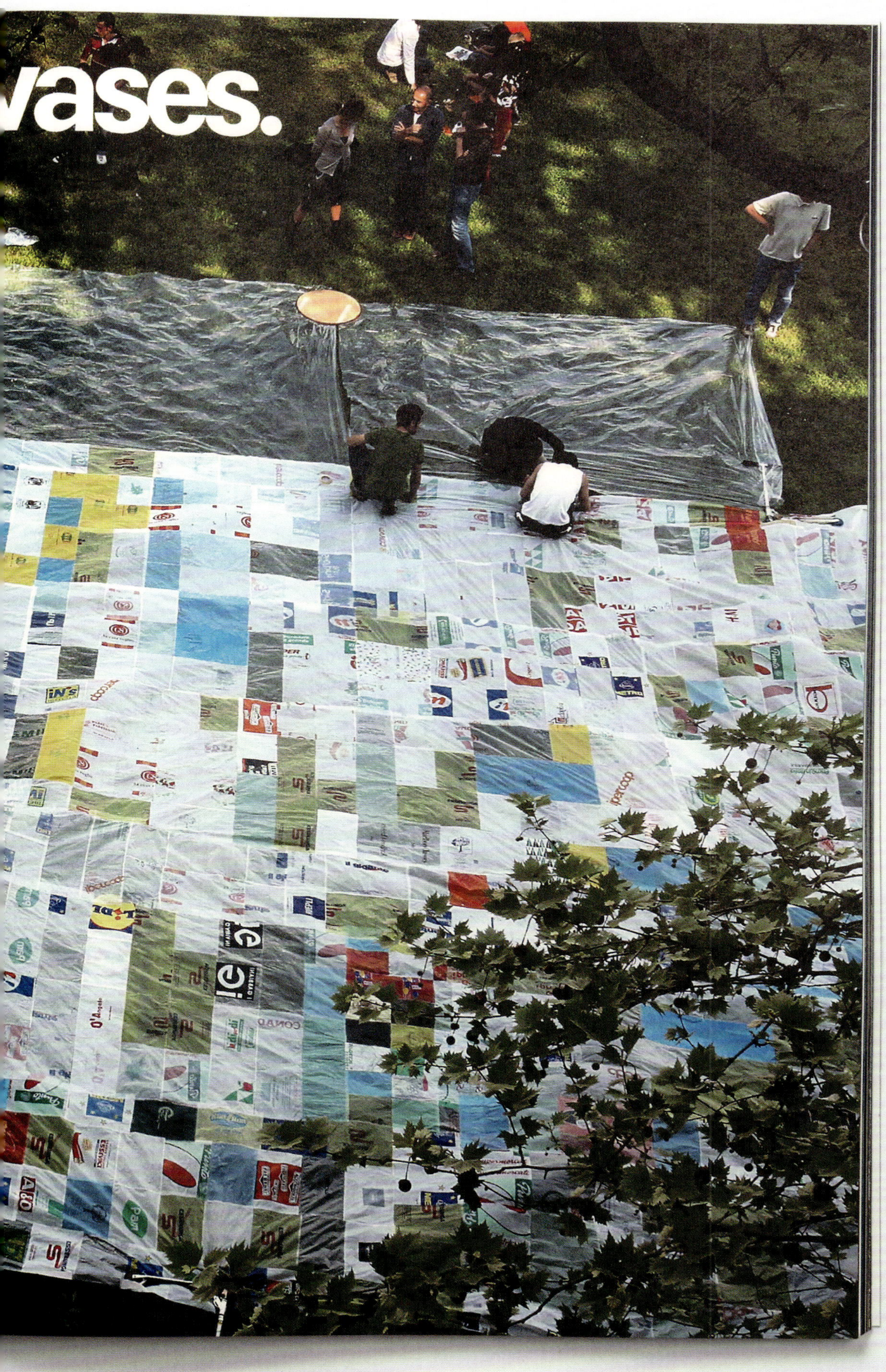

vases.

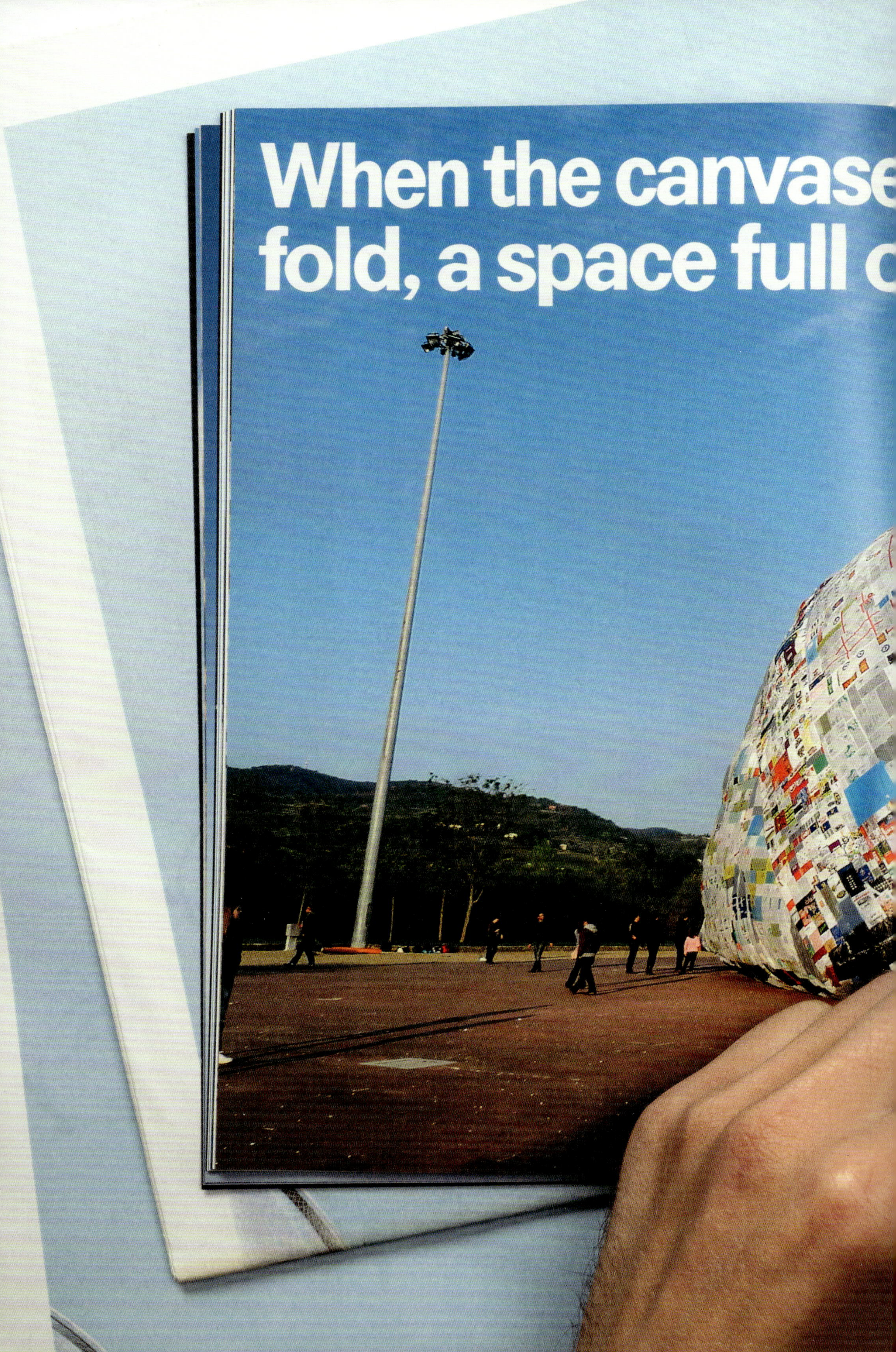

When the canvases
fold, a space full o

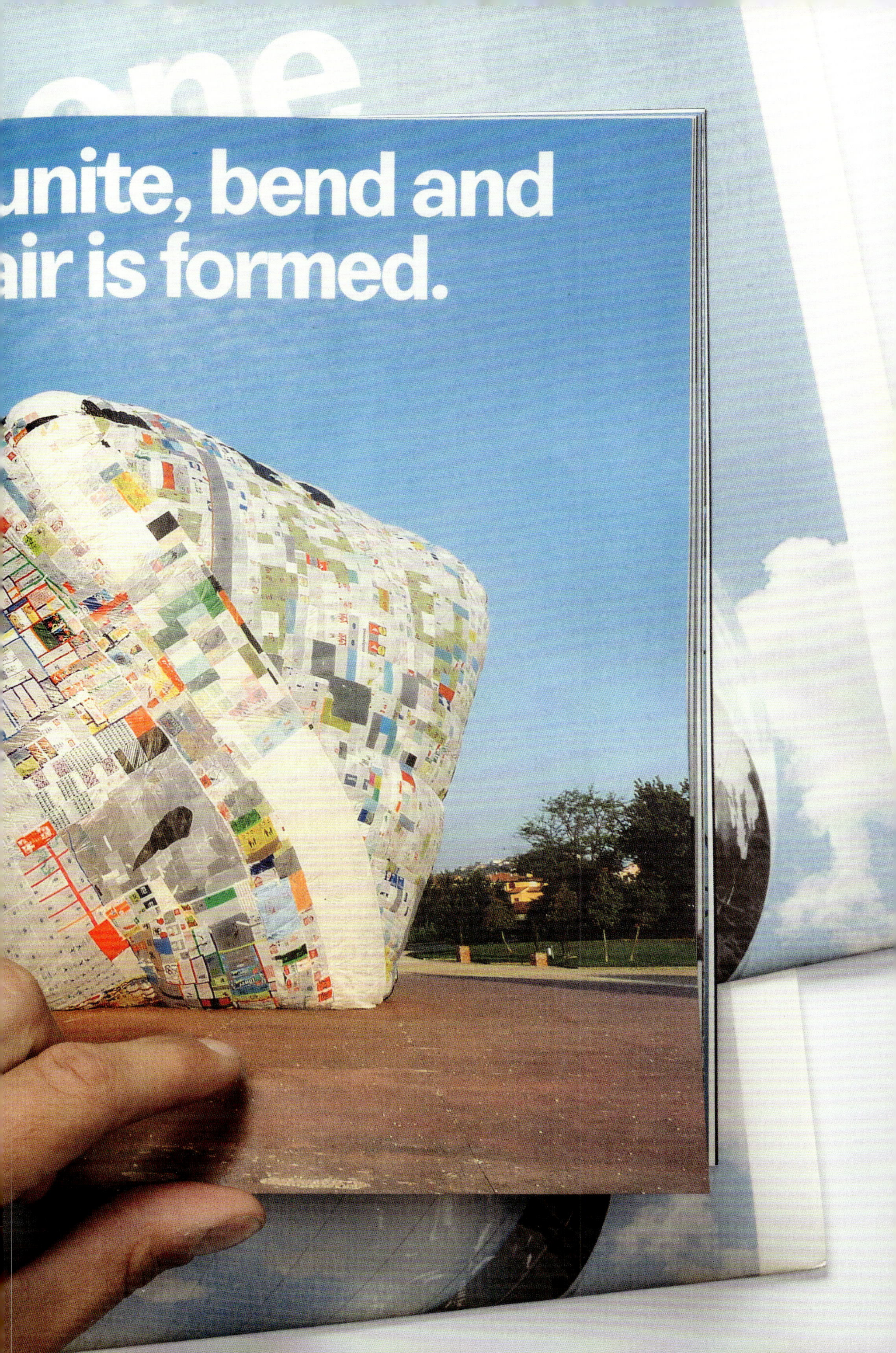
one
unite, bend and
air is formed.

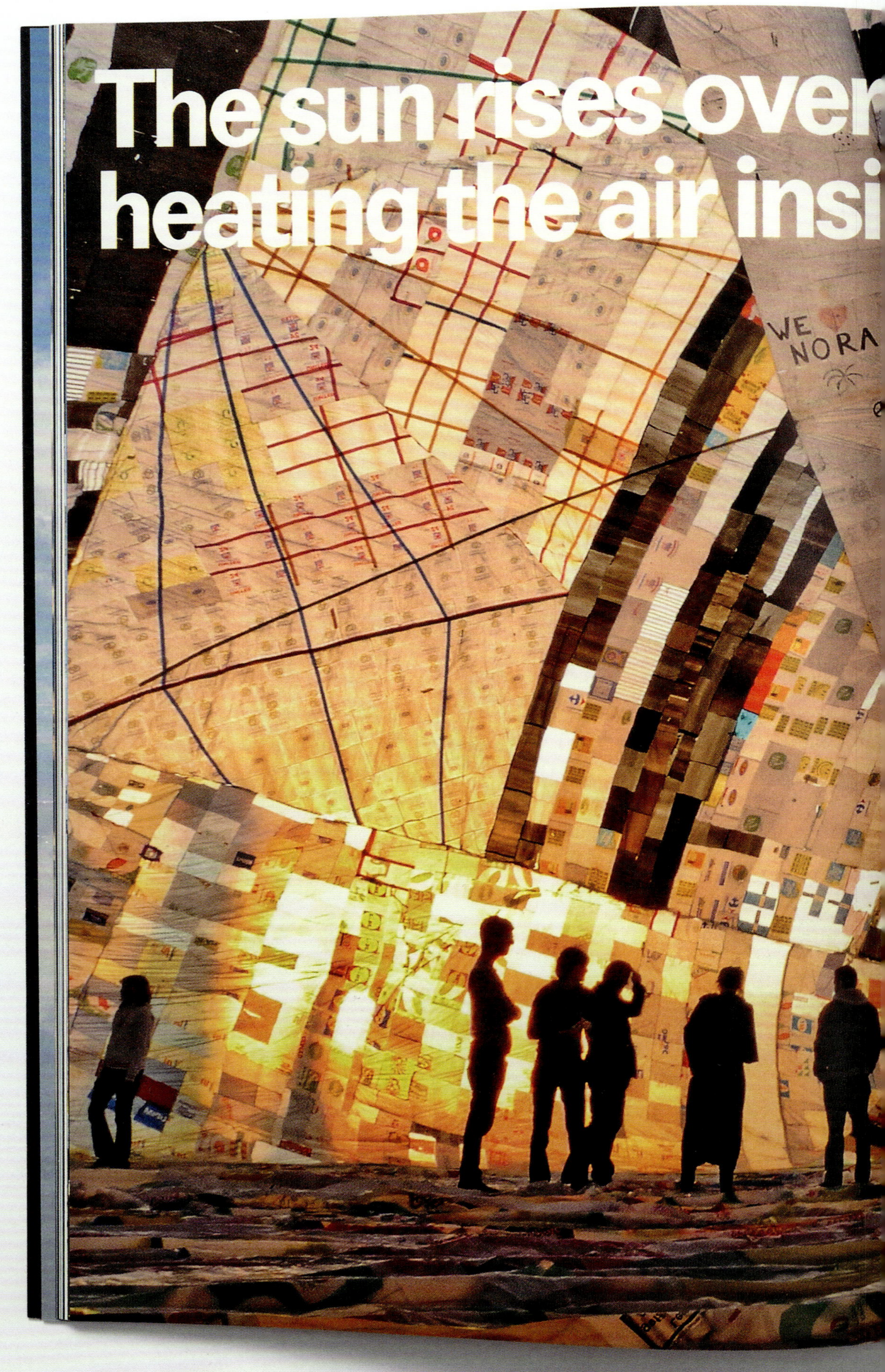
The sun rises over
heating the air insi
WE NORA

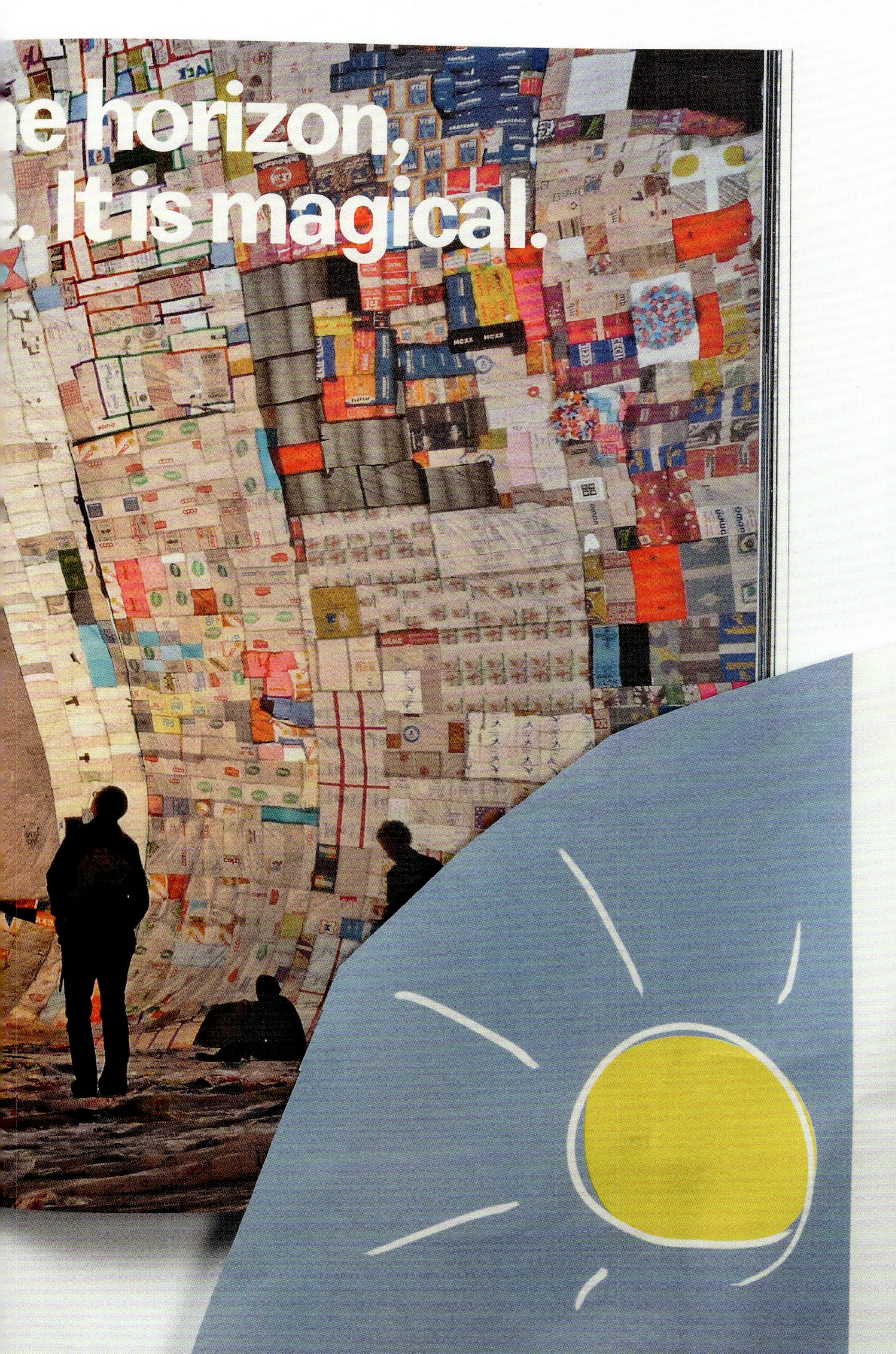
e horizon,
. It is magical.

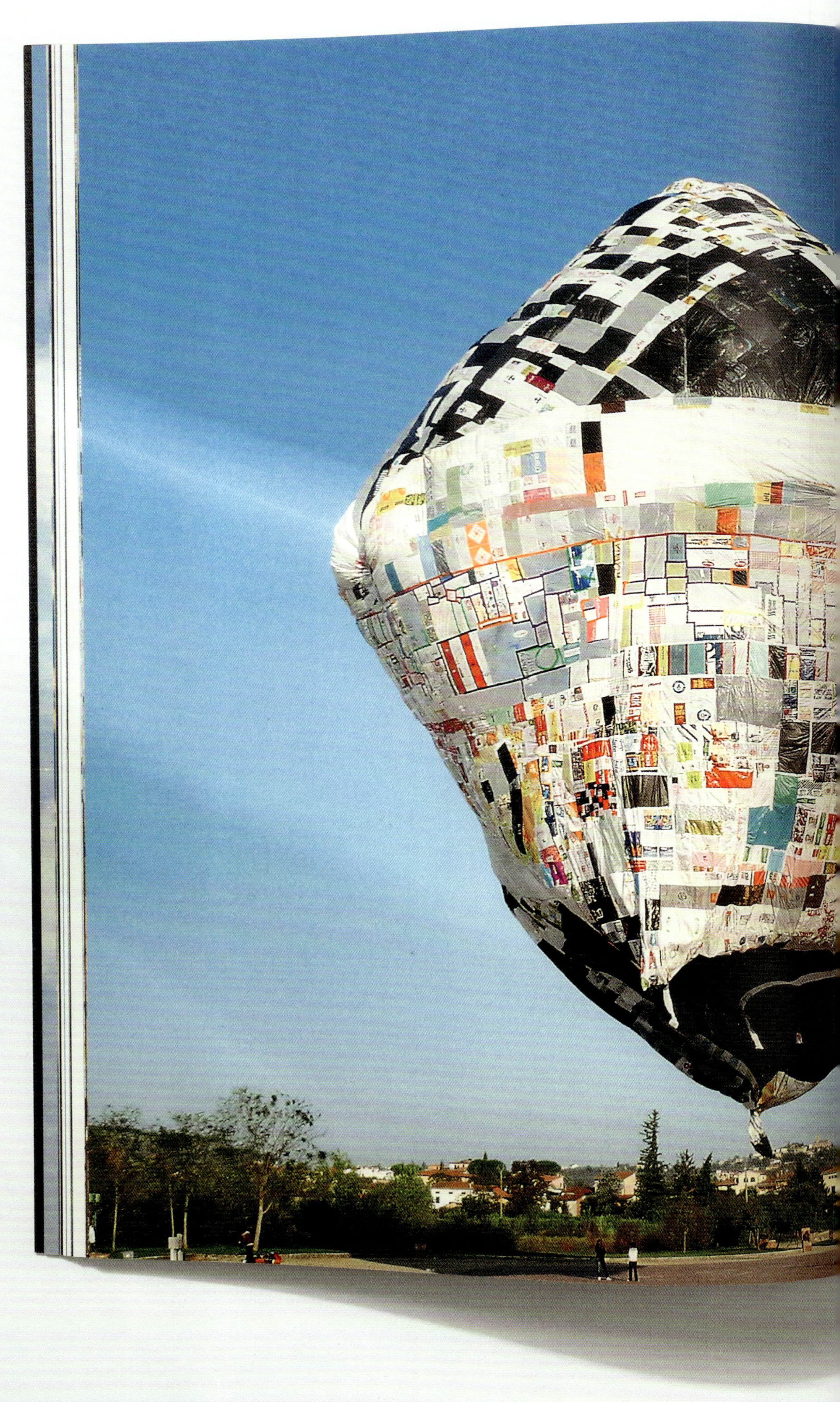

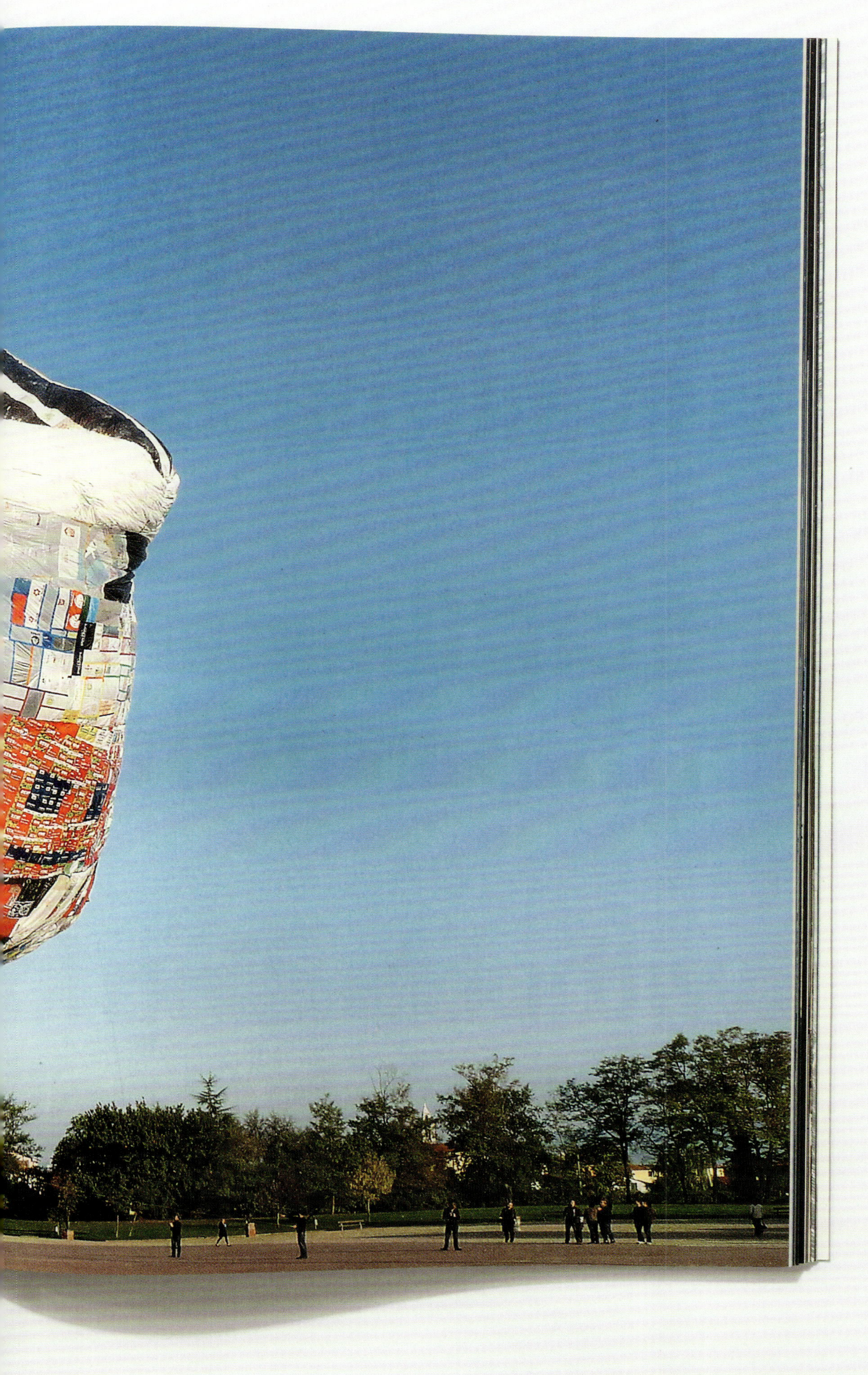

We call it
Museo Aer
a flying museum

From this idea w
in the air in a rad

without using fo
through our coll

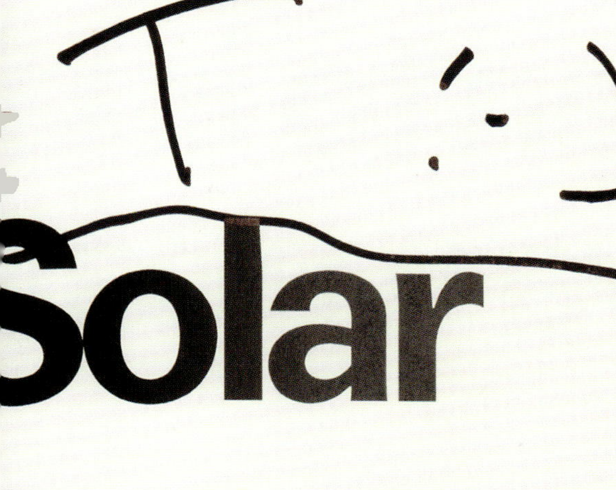

solar

earned to float
lly new way:

il fuels and
tive action.

We began to imagine
a new era we call
Aerocene

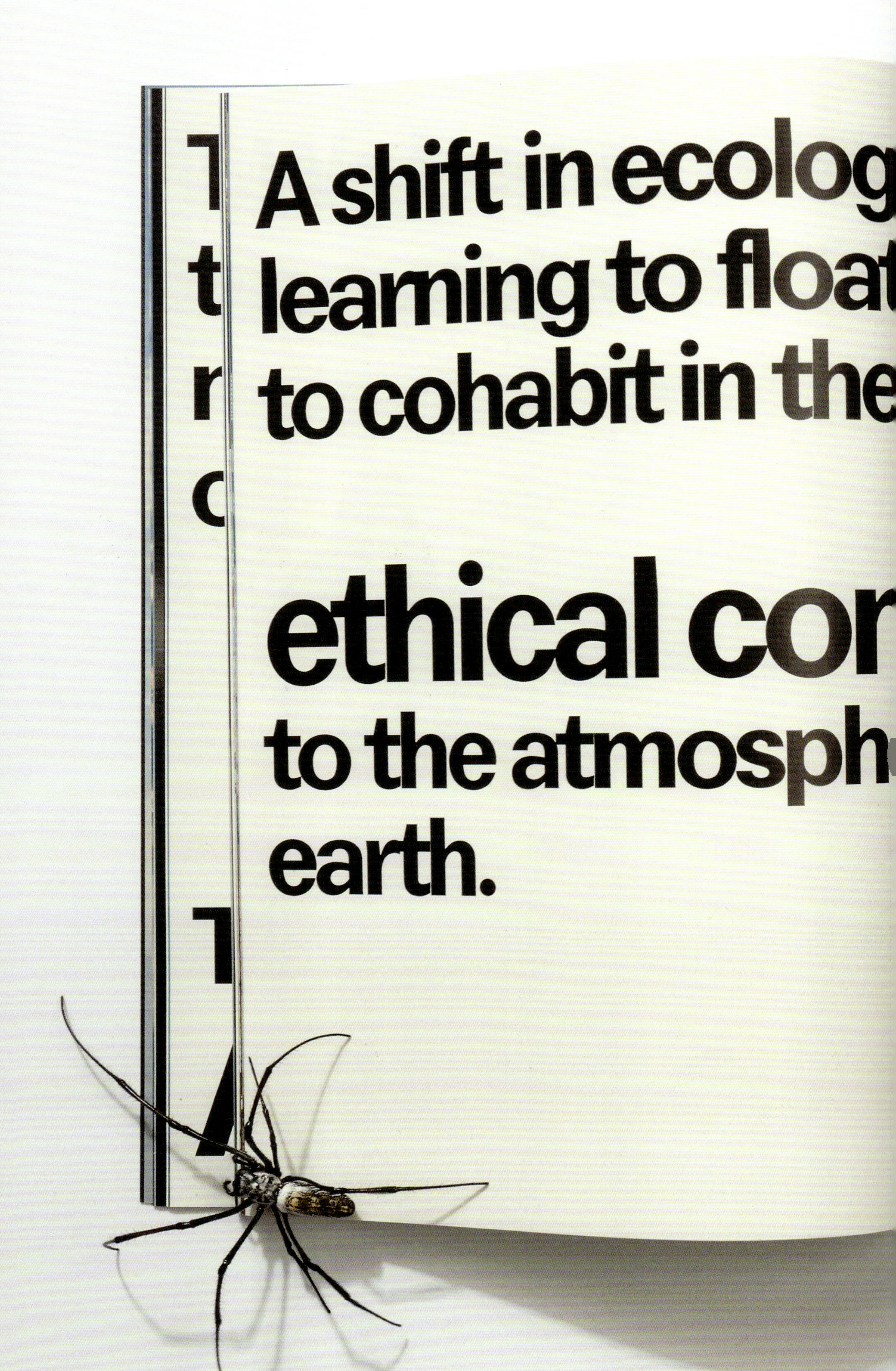
A shift in ecolog
learning to float
to cohabit in the
ethical con
to the atmosph
earth.

al awareness,
ogether,
r, towards an

mitment
e and planet

We work towa

inde

from

fossil fu

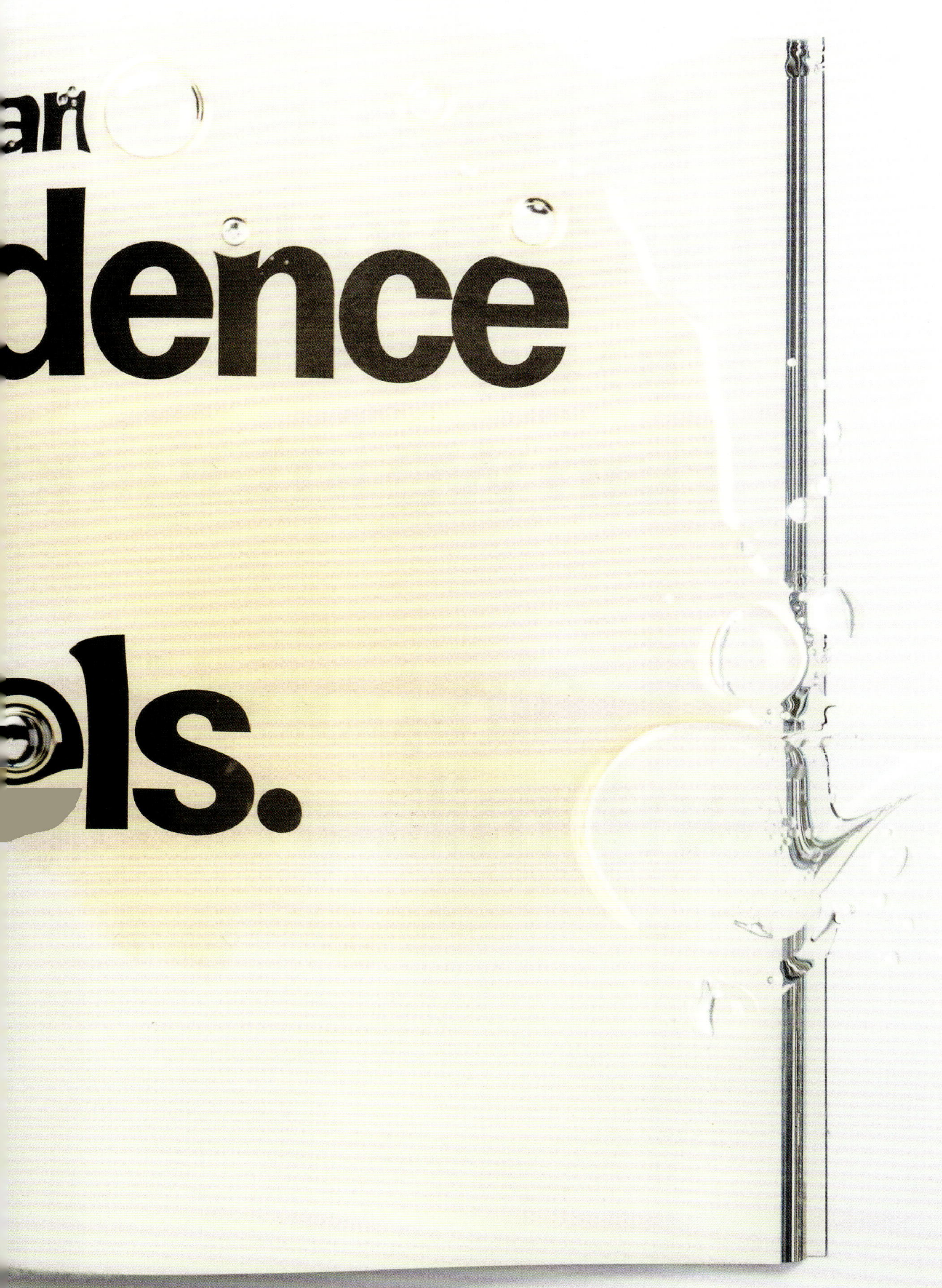

We have learned
but the journey t
the air is more c
than we imagine

the airspace is as
and militarized as

to float,
rough
mplicated

regulated
on the ground.

Air should belong t
Airspace should hav
The air we breathe i
we must preserve an

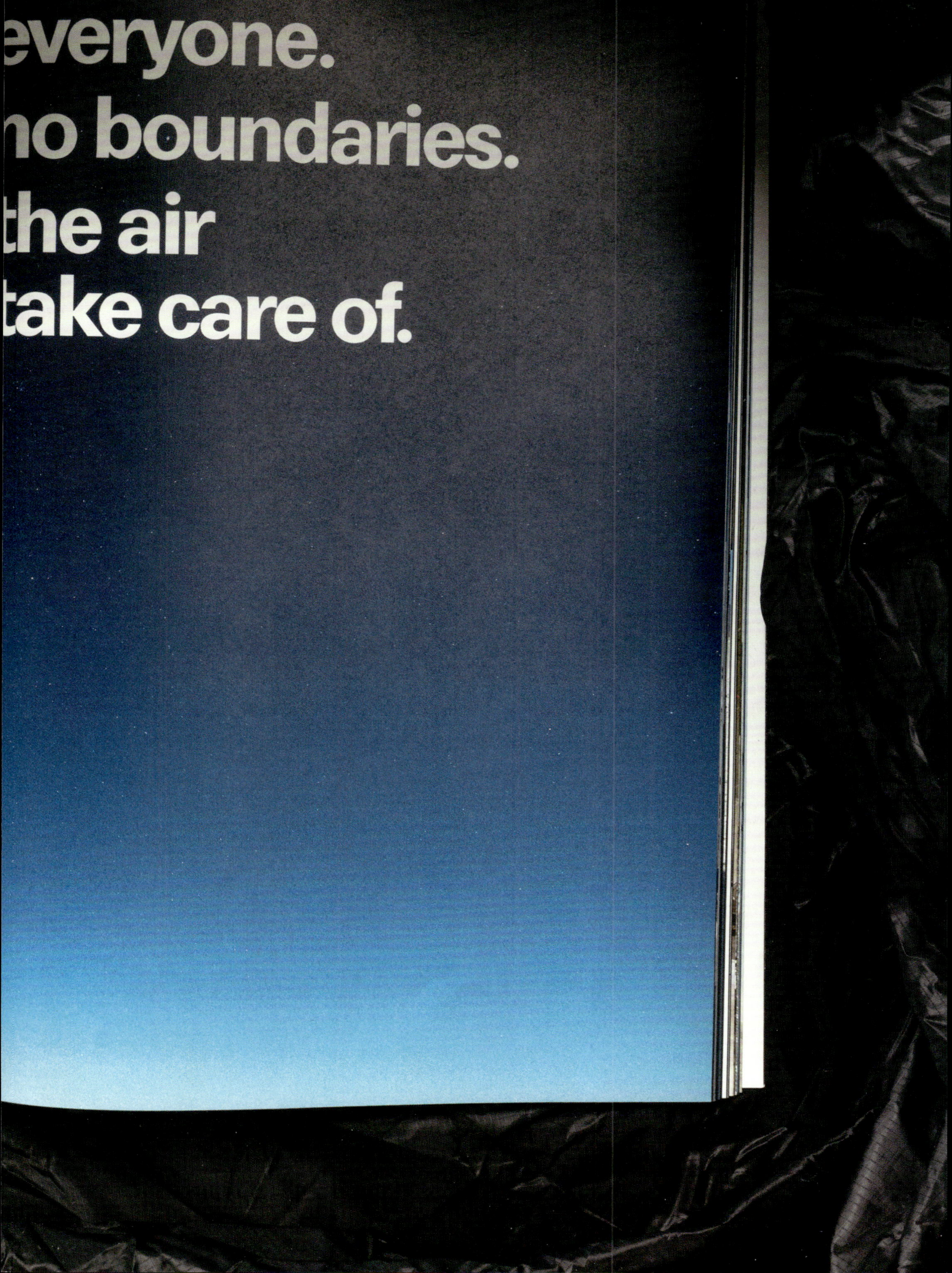

everyone.
no boundaries.
the air
take care of.

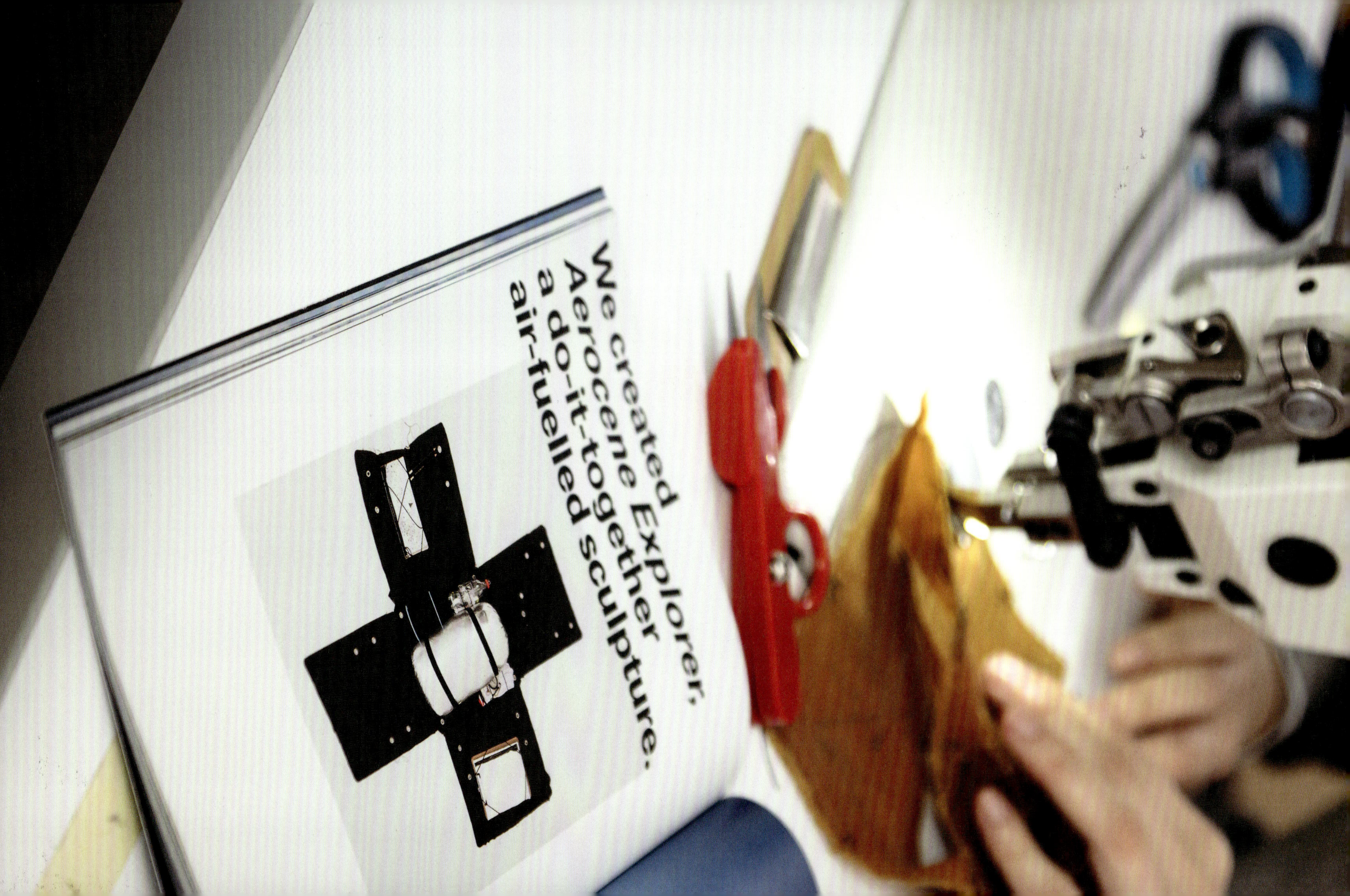

We created Explorer,
Aerocene
a do-it-together
air-fuelled sculpture.

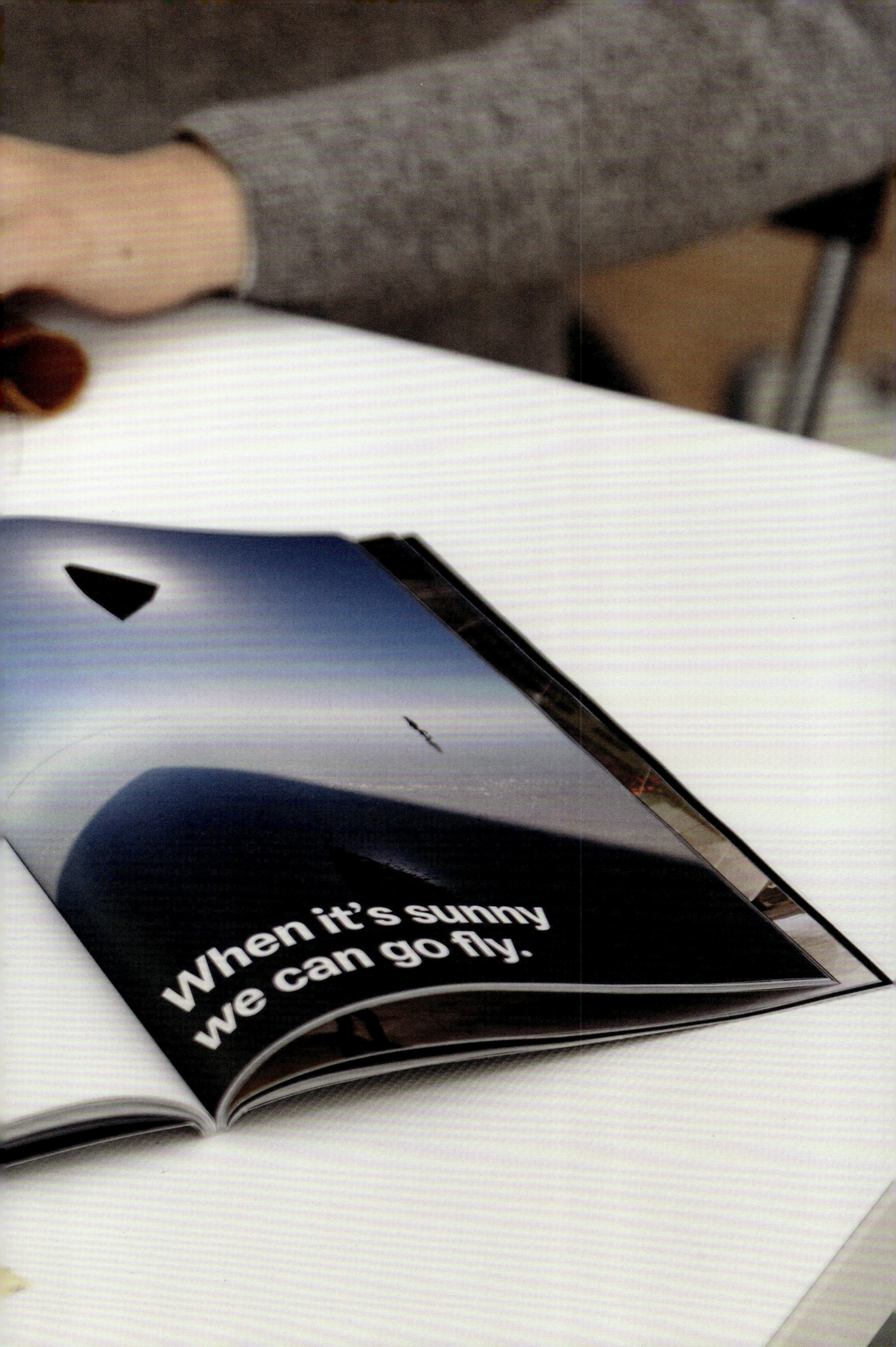

When it's sunny
we can go fly.

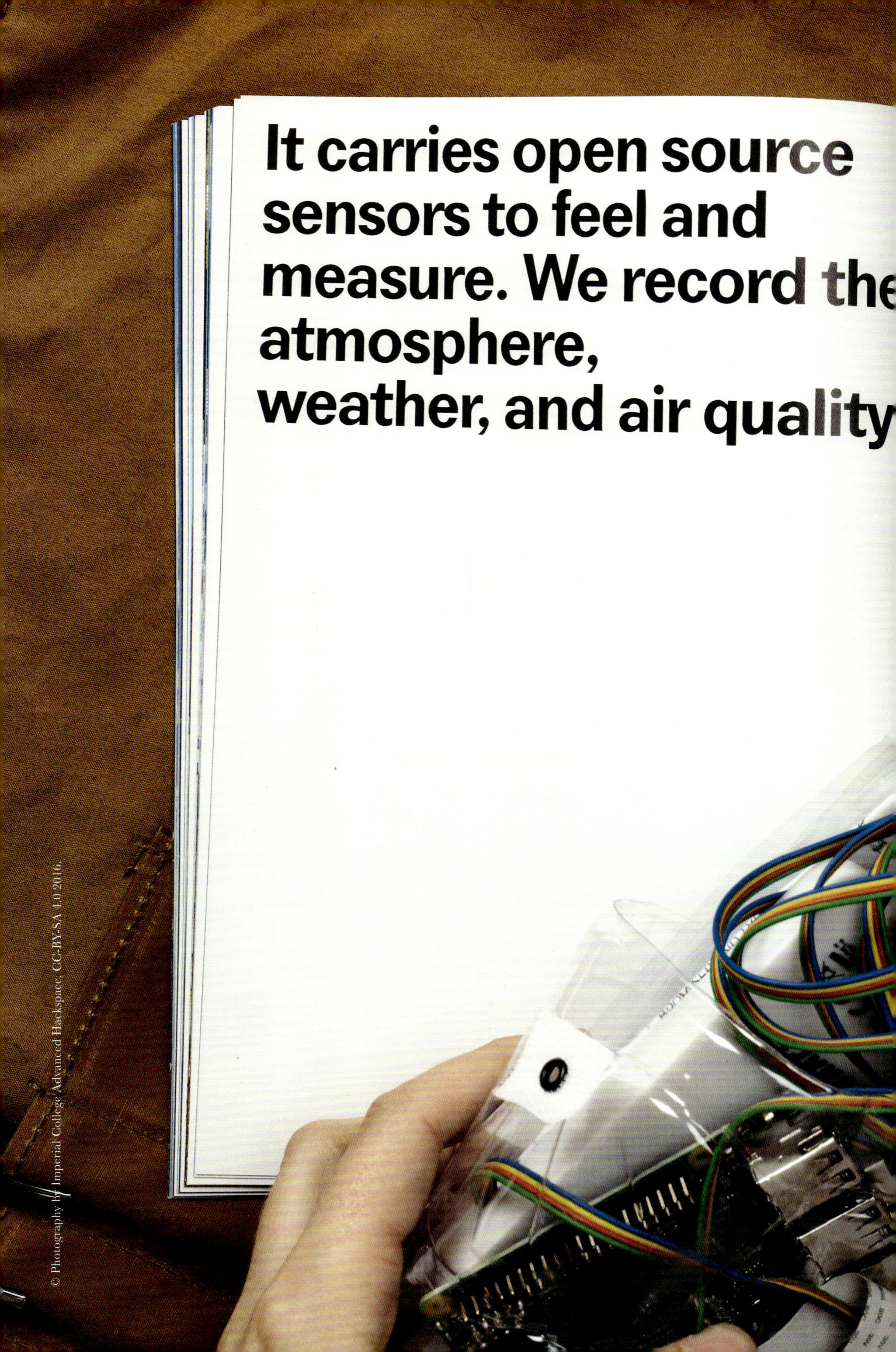

It carries open source
sensors to feel and
measure. We record the
atmosphere,
weather, and air quality

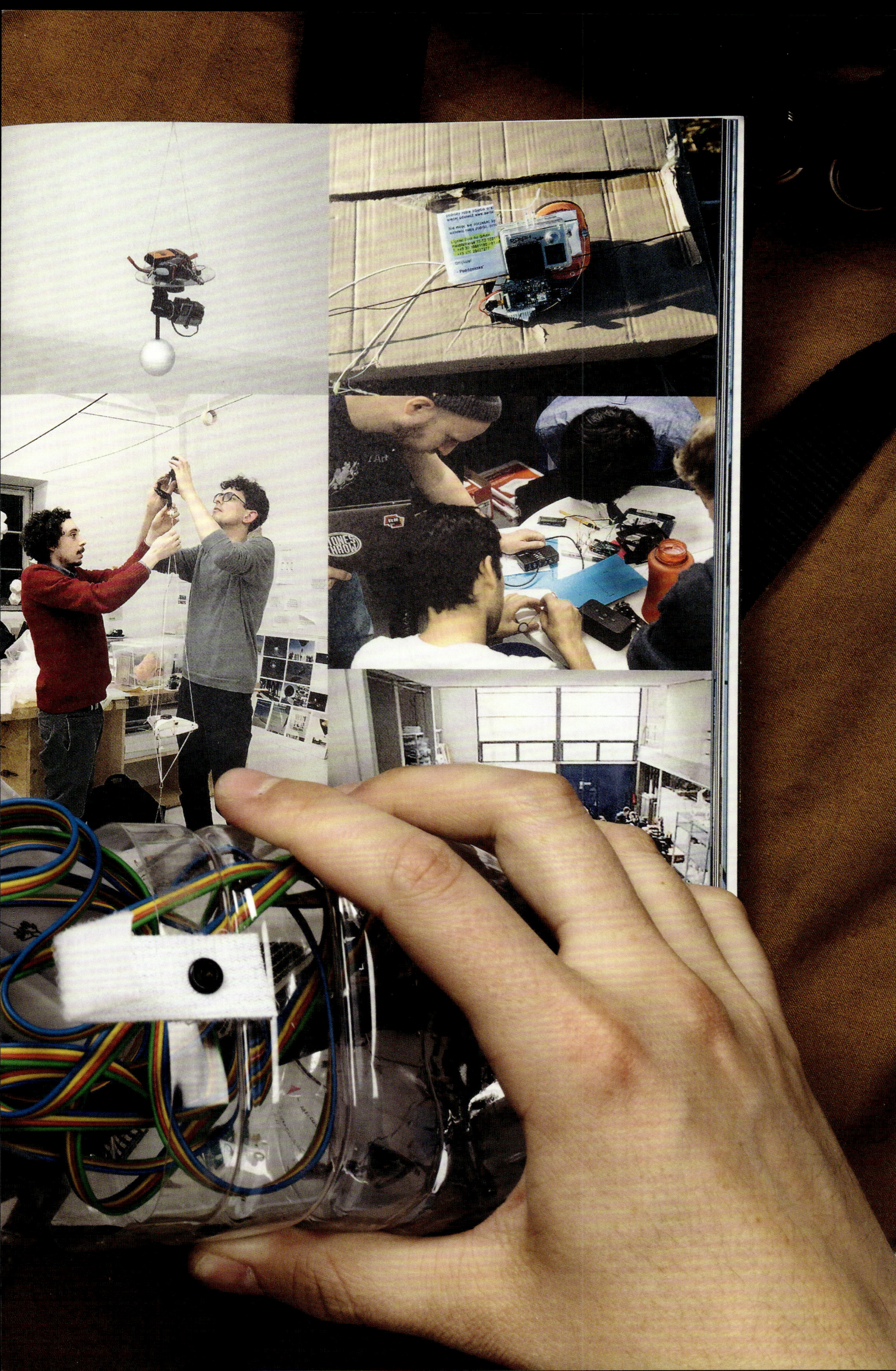

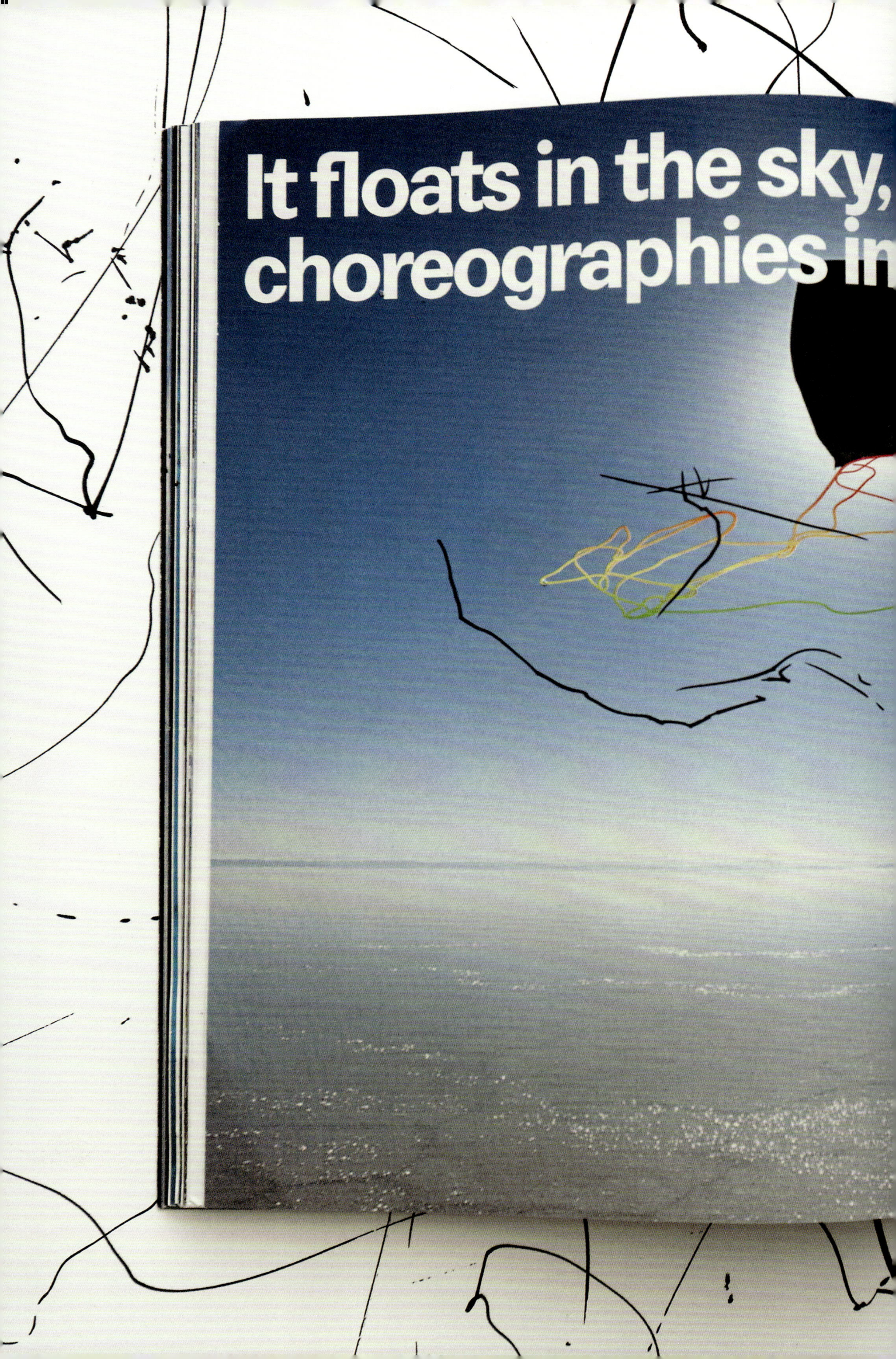

It floats in the sky,
choreographies in

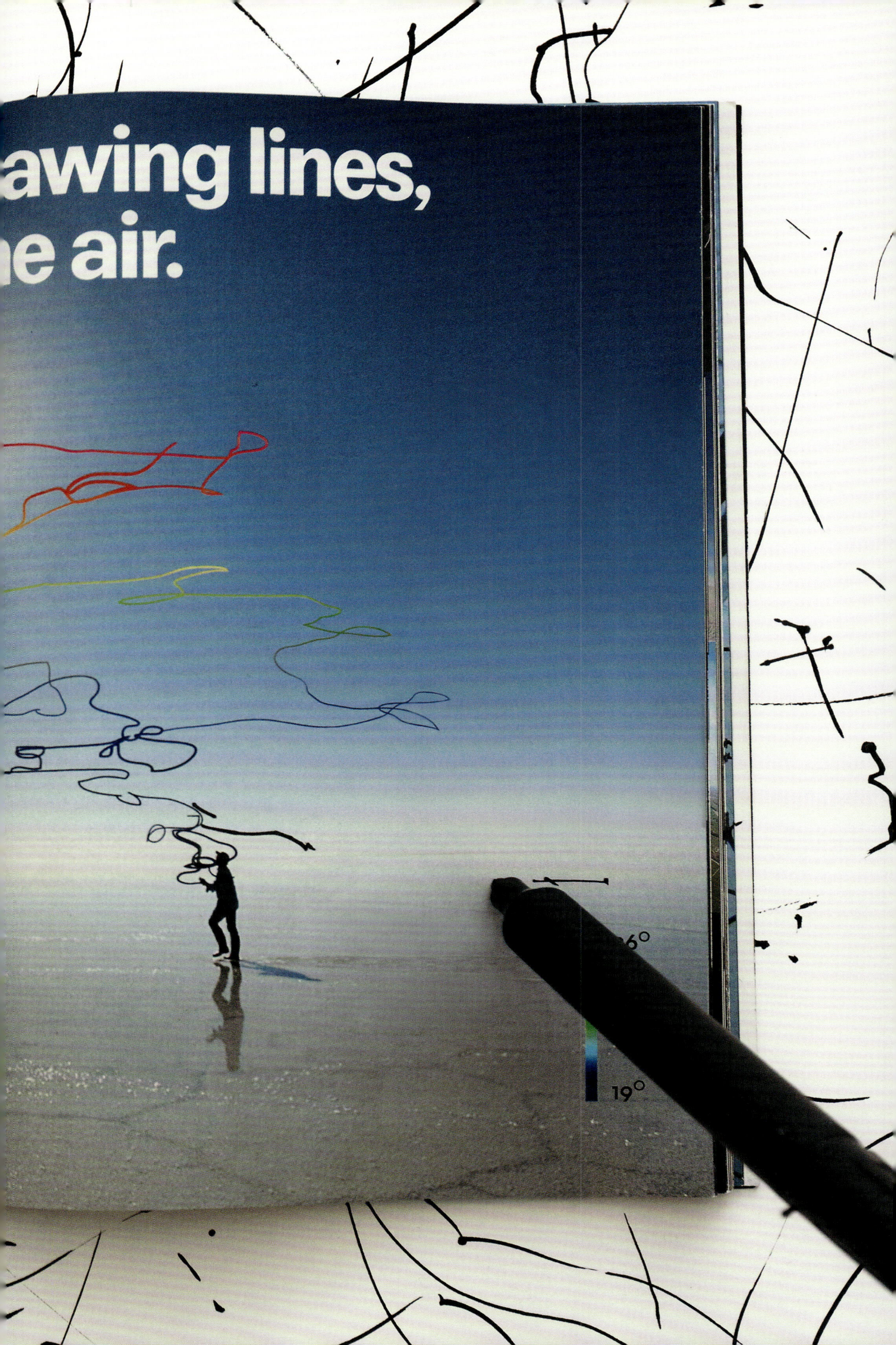
awing lines,
e air.
6°
19°

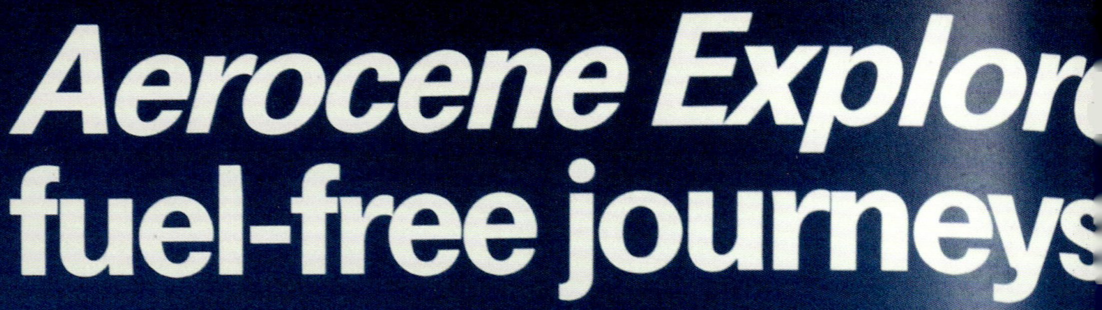

Aerocene Explore
fuel-free journeys
605 kilometers in 12 hours
54°00'15.3"N 22°45'33.2"E
Poland

has taken many
crossing borders.

52°27'32.4"N 14°03'15.3"E
Schönfelde 15518
Steinhöfel, Germany

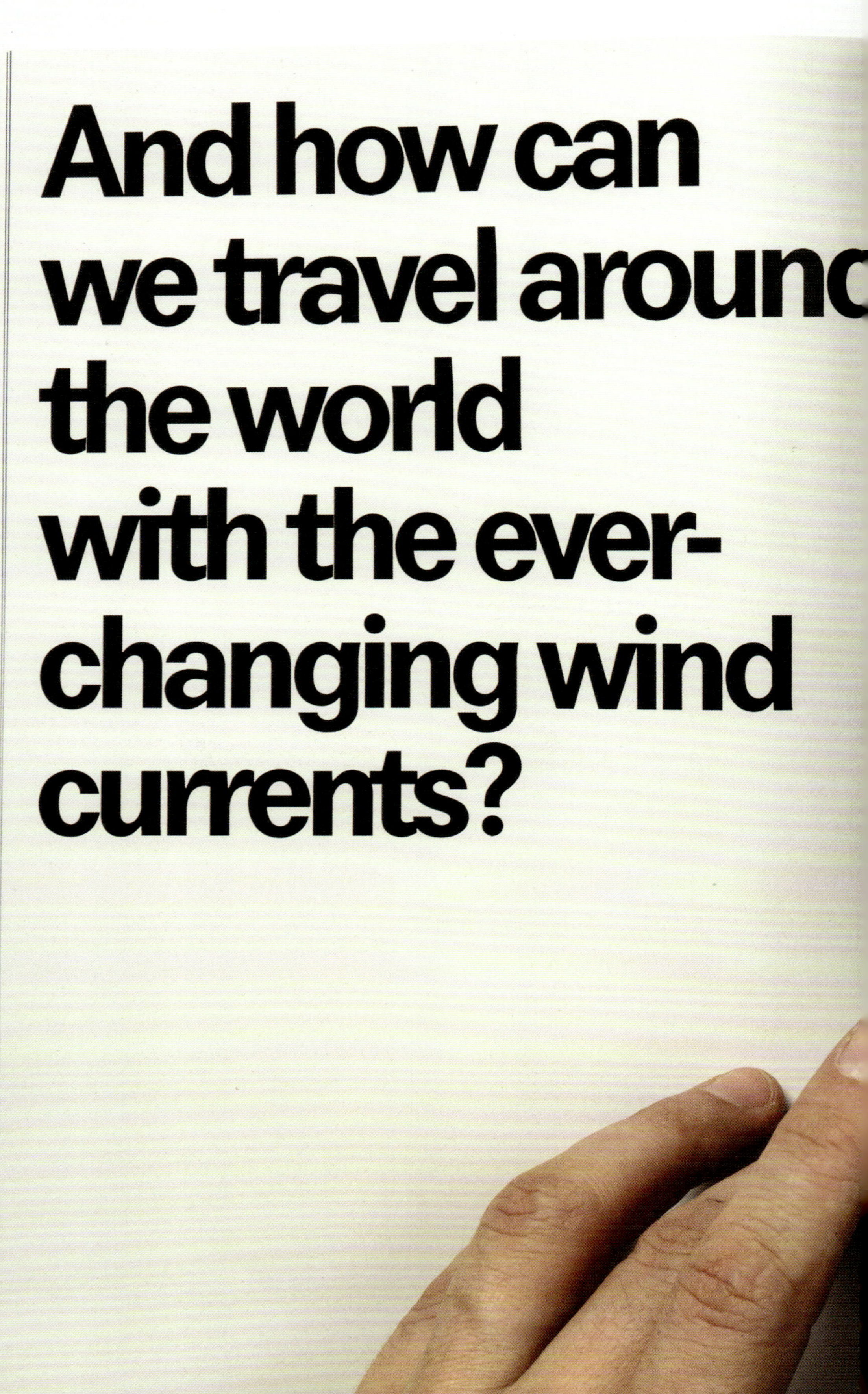

And how can we travel around the world with the ever-changing wind currents?

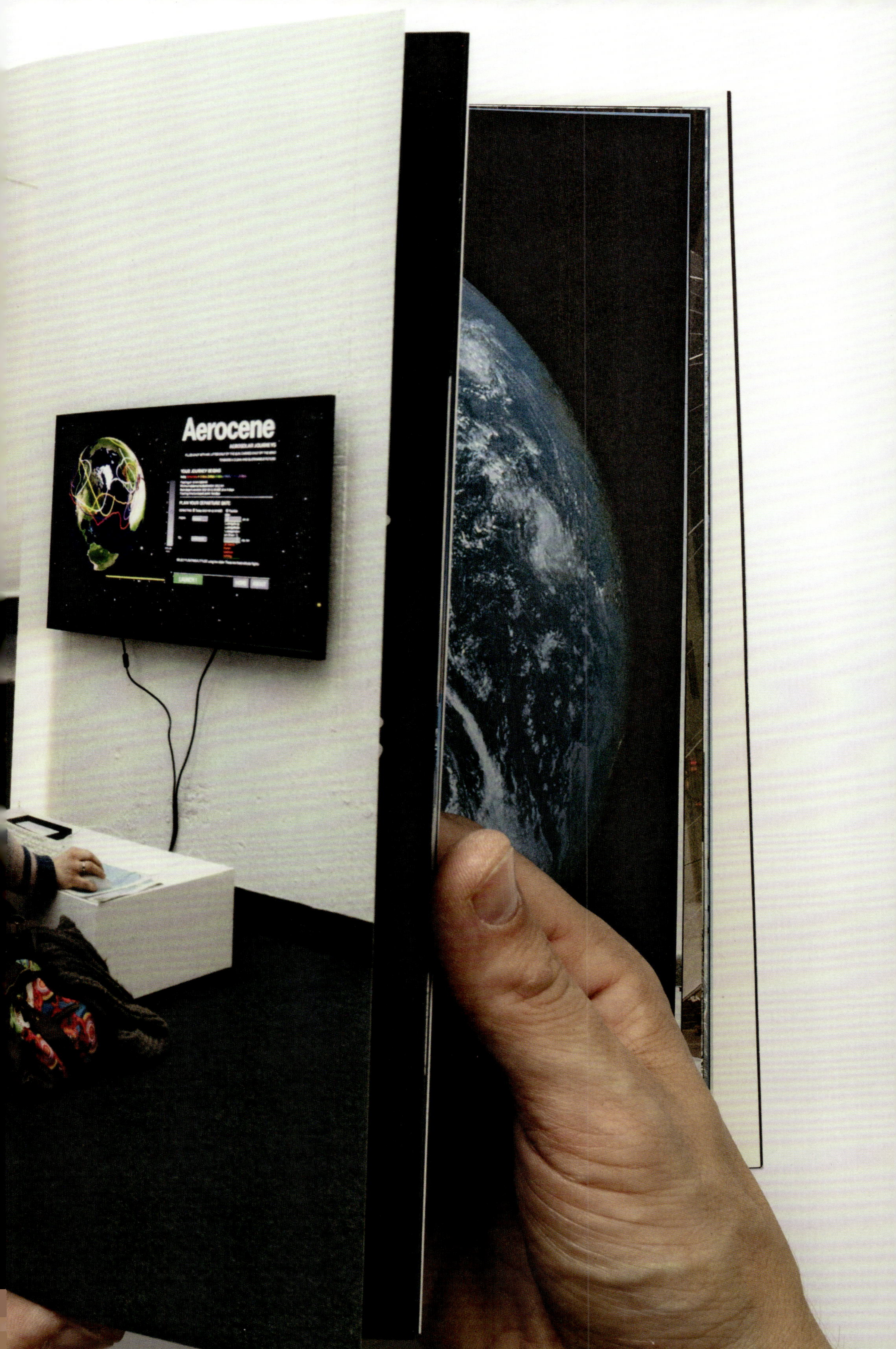
Aerocene

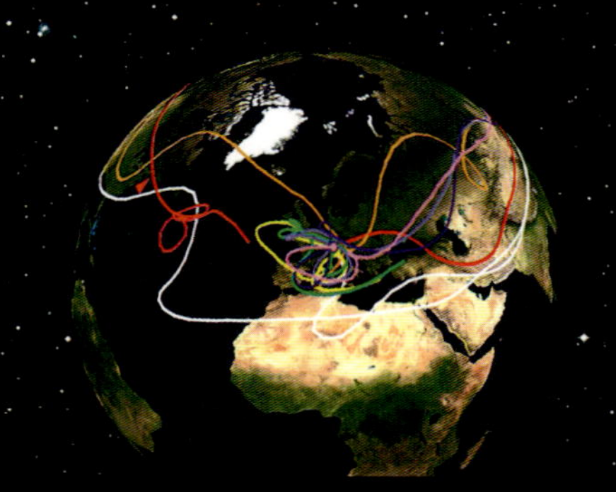

FOSSIL FUELS.
TEST YOUR AEROSOLAR JOURNEY WITH THE FLOAT PREDICTOR
Aerocene
AEROSOLAR JOURNEYS
INFLATED ONLY BY AIR, LIFTED ONLY BY THE SUN, CARRIED ONLY BY THE WIND
TOWARDS A CLEAN AND SUSTAINABLE FUTURE
PLAN YOUR JOURNEY -- DEPARTURE DATES
DEPARTING: Today (2017-01-12 00:00Z) Flexible date
FROM: Switzerland Davos
TO: United States Boston
Click on globe to select locations or enter country and city.
SELECT FLOATING ALTITUDE using the slider. This mode calculates only fixed-altitude flight.
Changing wind speed and direction means departure time can significantly affect the flight path. You will see eight trajectories starting from the same spot, but launched on successive days.
Color-coded by departure date
today, tomorrow, 2 days, 3 days, 4 days, 5 days, 7 days.
YOUR TRIP
Flying at: 10 km (250mb)
float.aerocene.org

Together with MIT, we have developed the Float Predictor, a website that can calculate how the wind can take you anywhere. To travel from one place to another, you first choose an altitude; different altitudes allow for different directions and speeds.

These trajectories become signatures supporting our work towards an independence from fossil fuels.

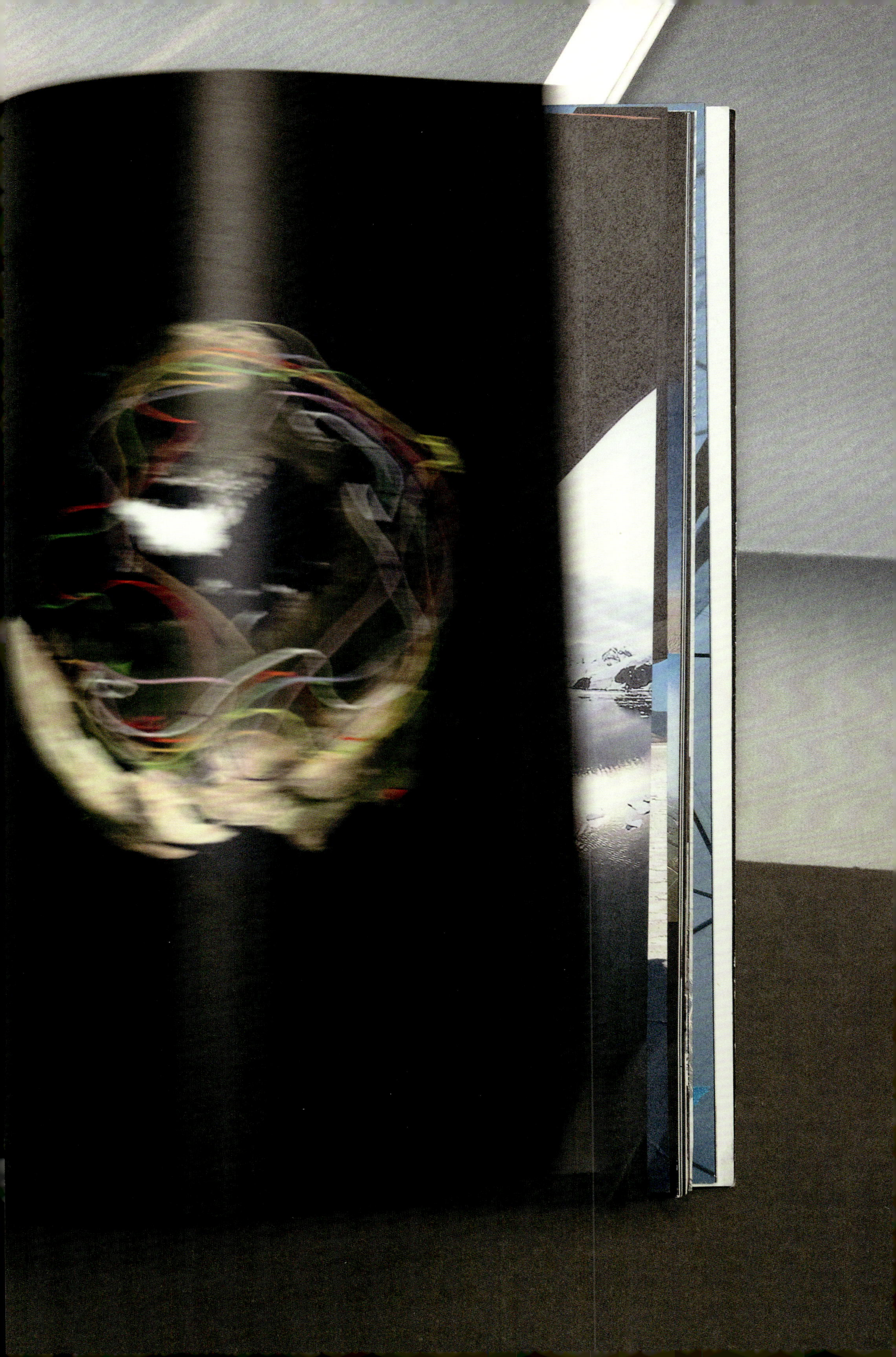

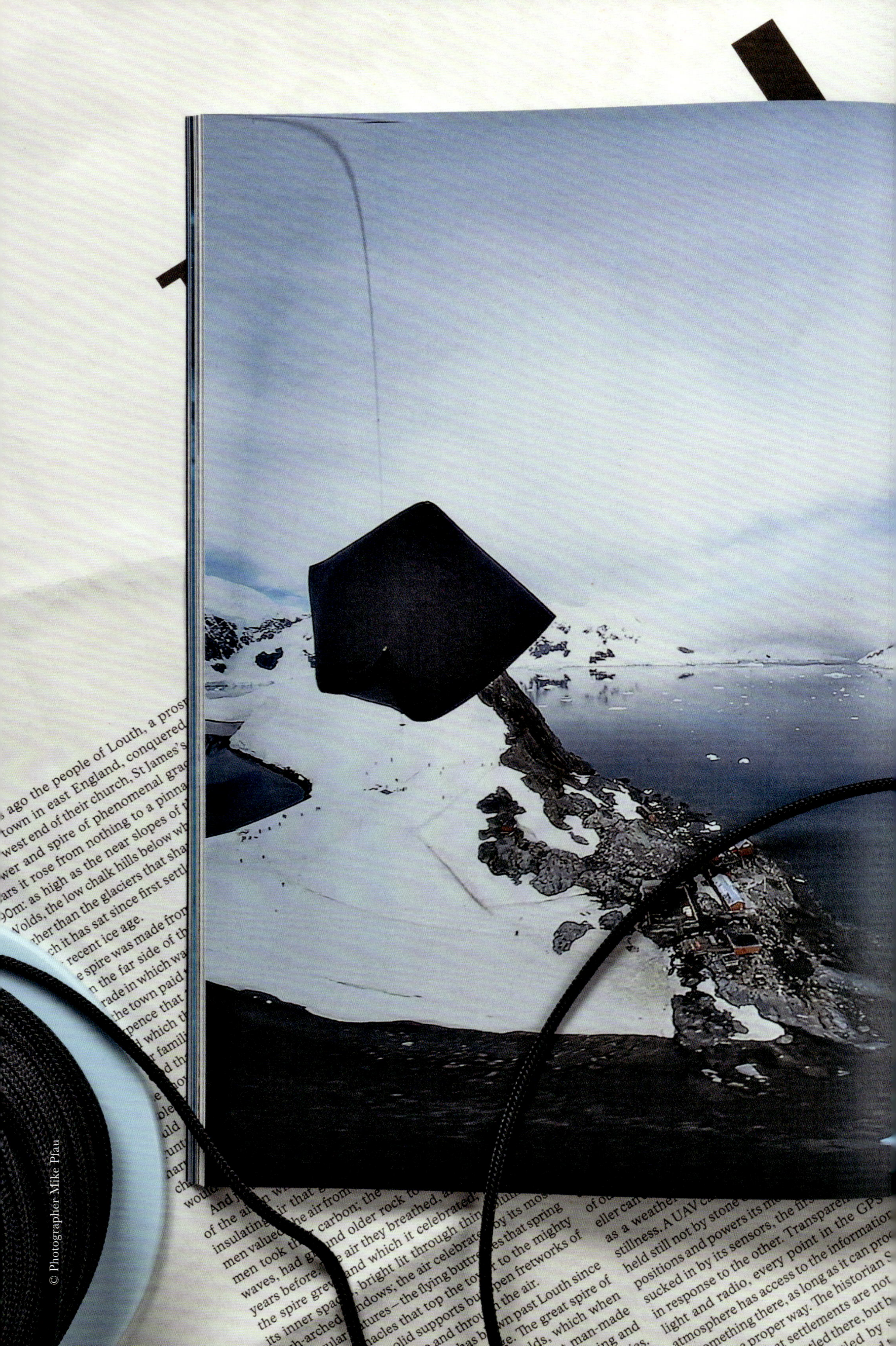

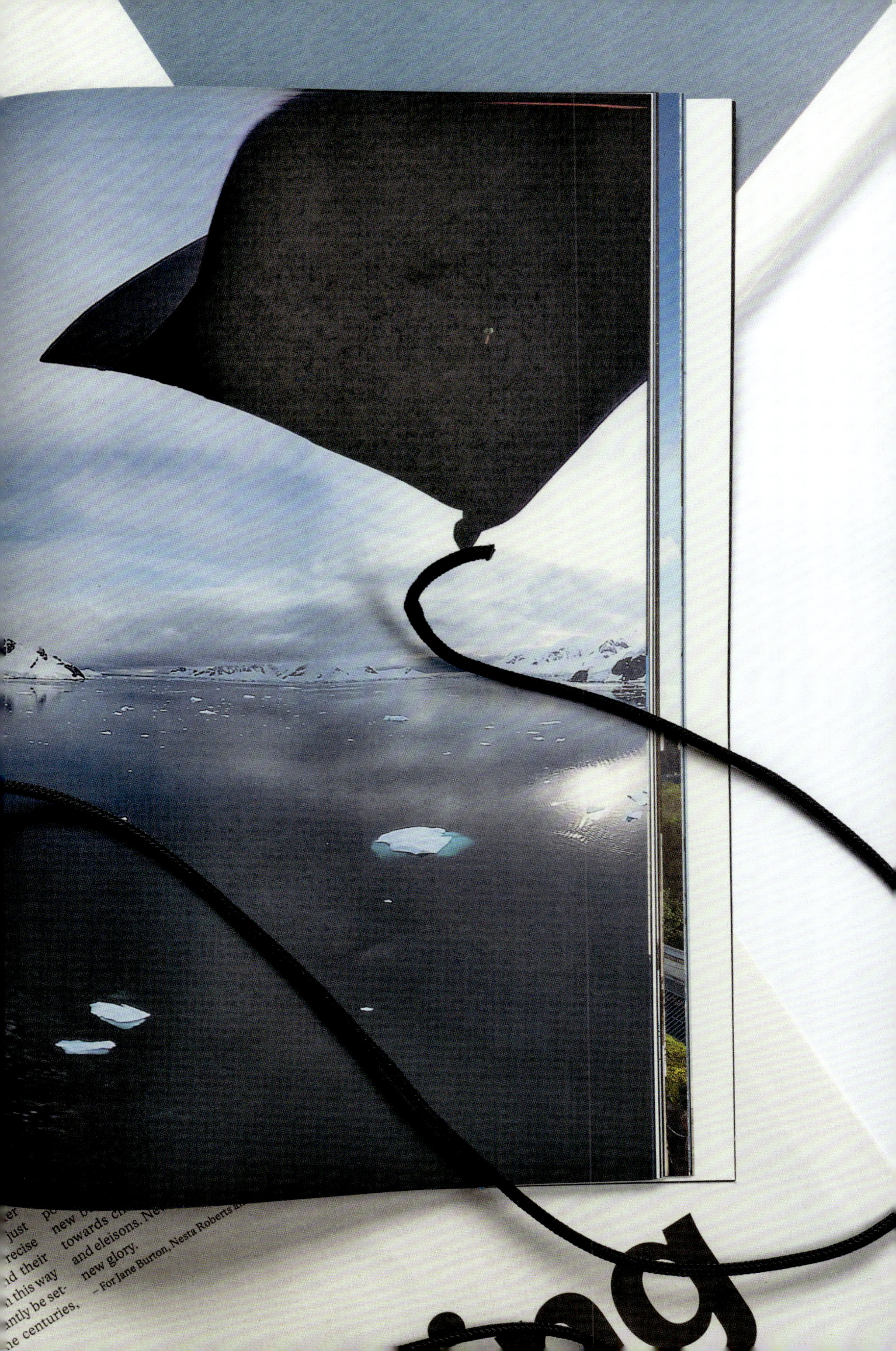
just
recise   new
their   towards
this way   and eleisons. Ne
ntly be set-   new glory.
centuries,   — For Jane Burton, Nesta Roberts

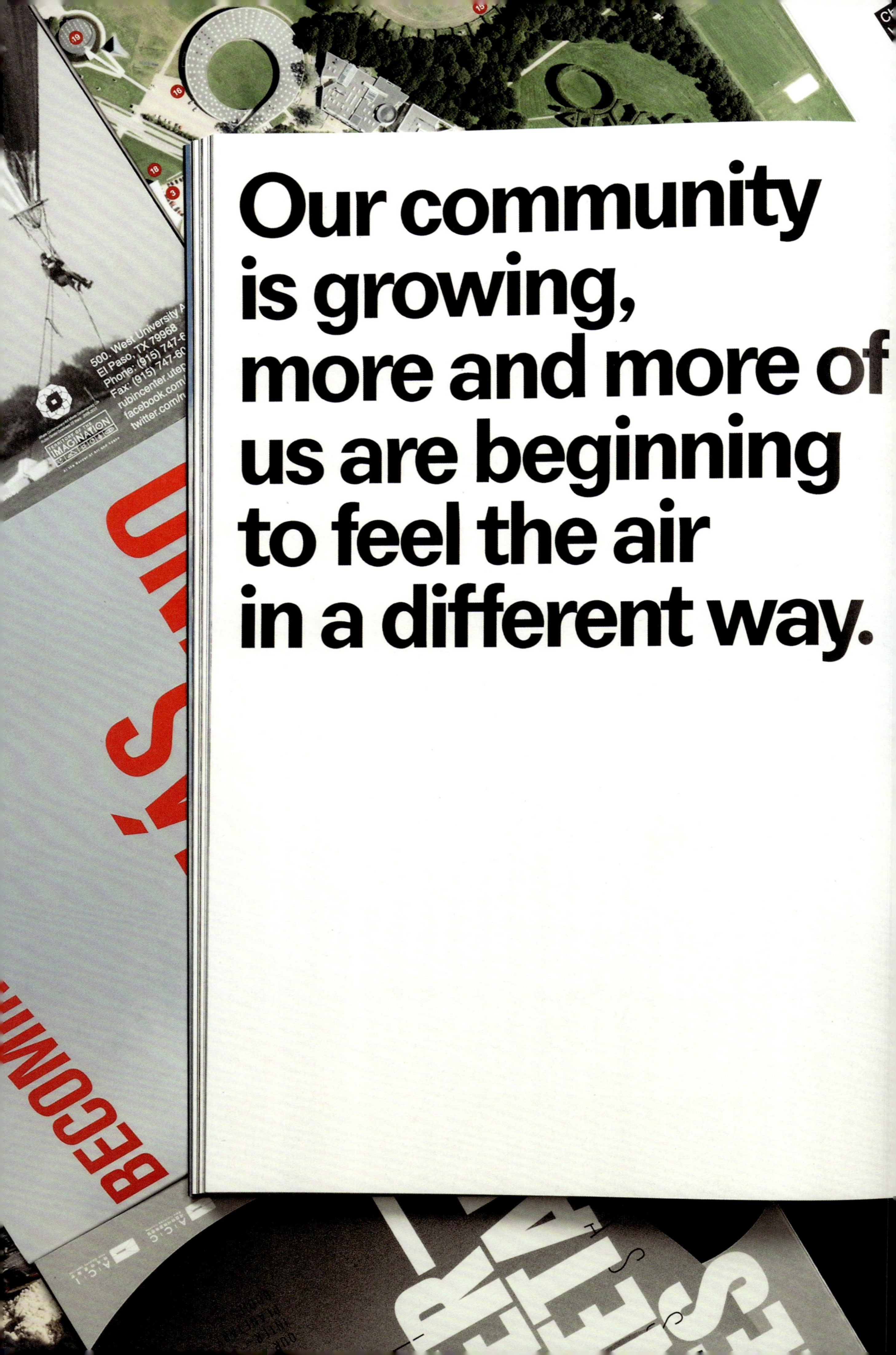
Our community
is growing,
more and more of
us are beginning
to feel the air
in a different way.
500. West University A
El Paso, TX 79968
Phone: (915) 747-
Fax: (915) 747-6
rubincenter.com
facebook.com
twitter.com/

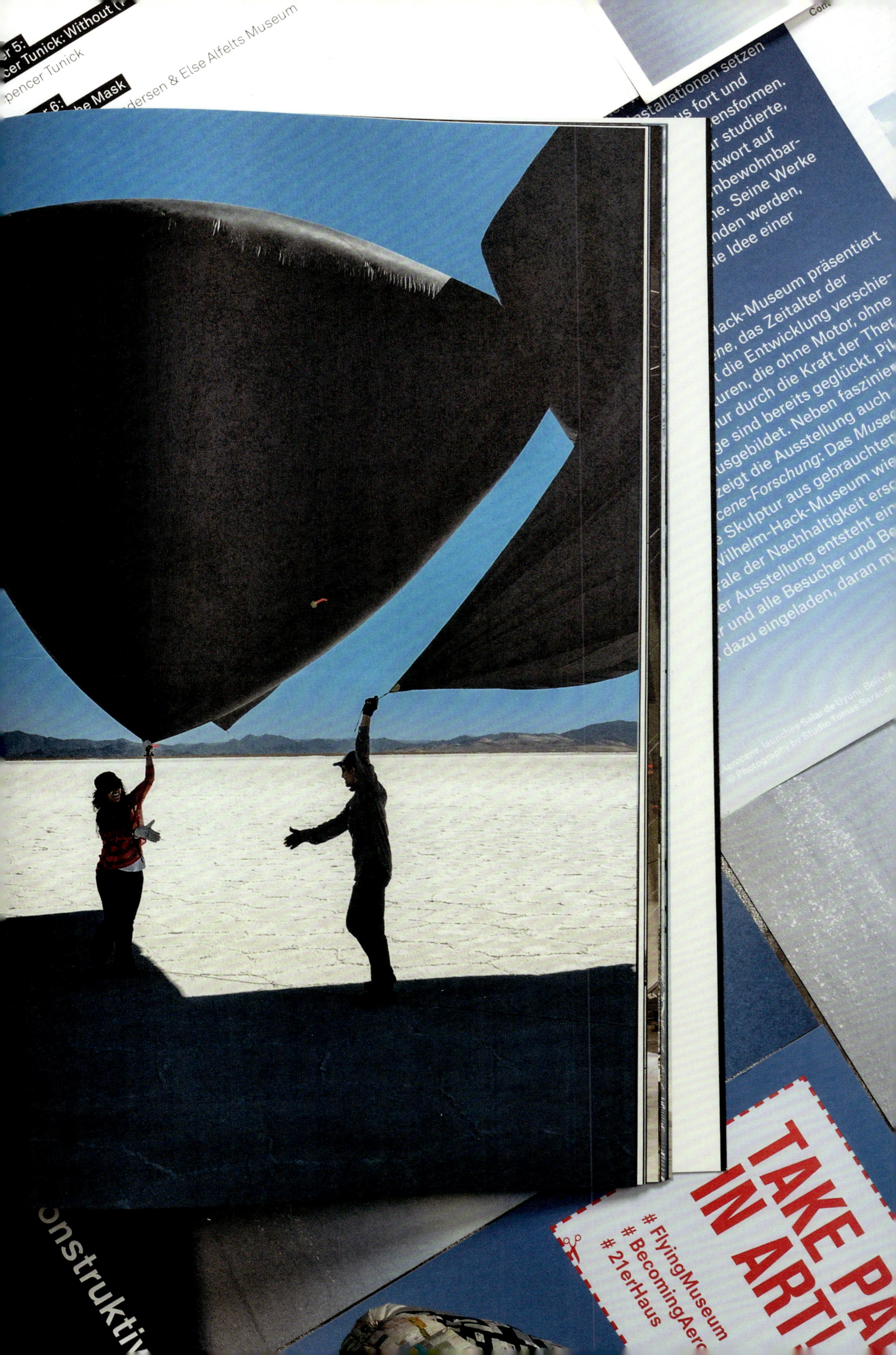

er 5:
cer Tunick: Without (
pencer Tunick
6:     he Mask
dersen & Else Alfelts Museum
stallationen setzen
us fort und
ensformen.
ar studierte,
twort auf
nbewohnbar-
e. Seine Werke
den werden,
ie Idee einer
ack-Museum präsentiert
ene, das Zeitalter der
die Entwicklung verschie-
uren, die ohne Motor, ohne
ur durch die Kraft der Ther
ge sind bereits geglückt, Pil
usgebildet. Neben faszinie
zeigt die Ausstellung auch
cene-Forschung: Das Muse
Skulptur aus gebrauchte
Wilhelm-Hack-Museum wie
rale der Nachhaltigkeit ers
er Ausstellung entsteht ei
r und alle Besucher und Be
dazu eingeladen, daran m
Aerocene, launches Salar de Uyuni, Bolivia.
© Photography by Studio Tomás Saracen
TAKE PA
IN ART
FlyingMuseum
BecomingAer
21erHaus

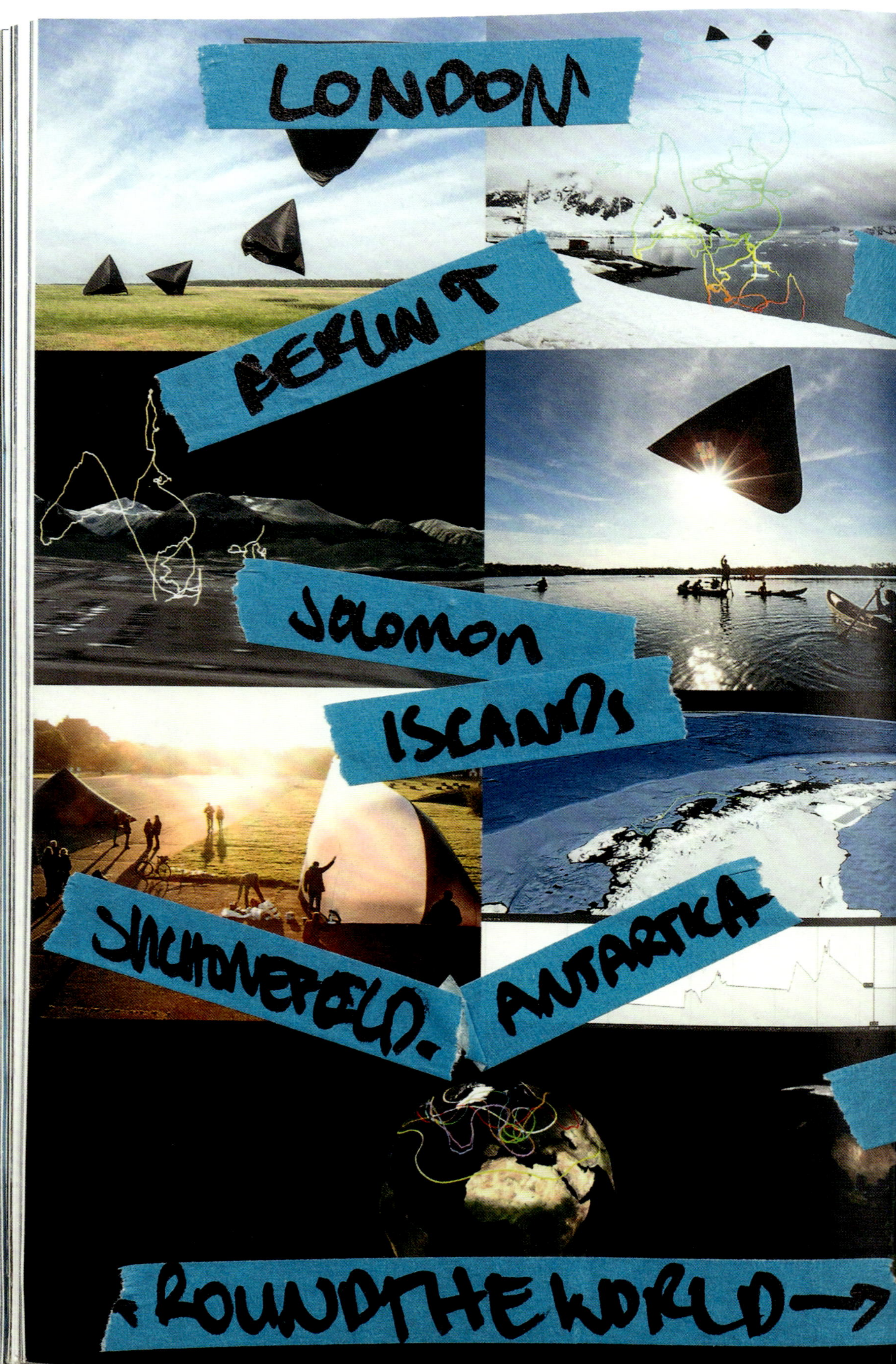

LONDON
BERLIN ?
SOLOMON ISLANDS
SCHÖNEFELD -
ANTARTICA
← ROUND THE WORLD →

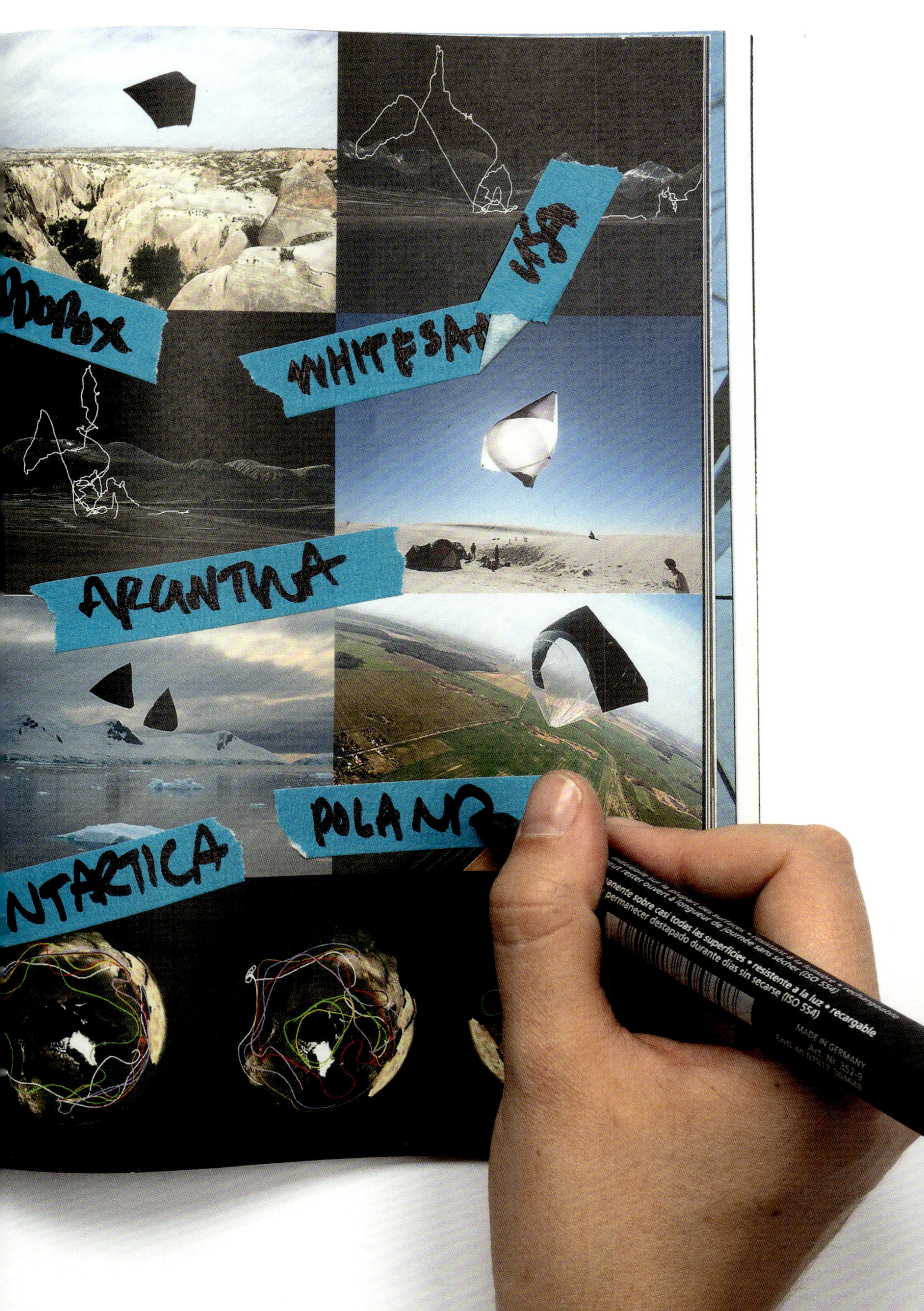
DOPOX
USA
WHITESAN
ARANTNA
ANTARTICA
POLAND
MADE IN GERMANY
Art. Nr. 352-9

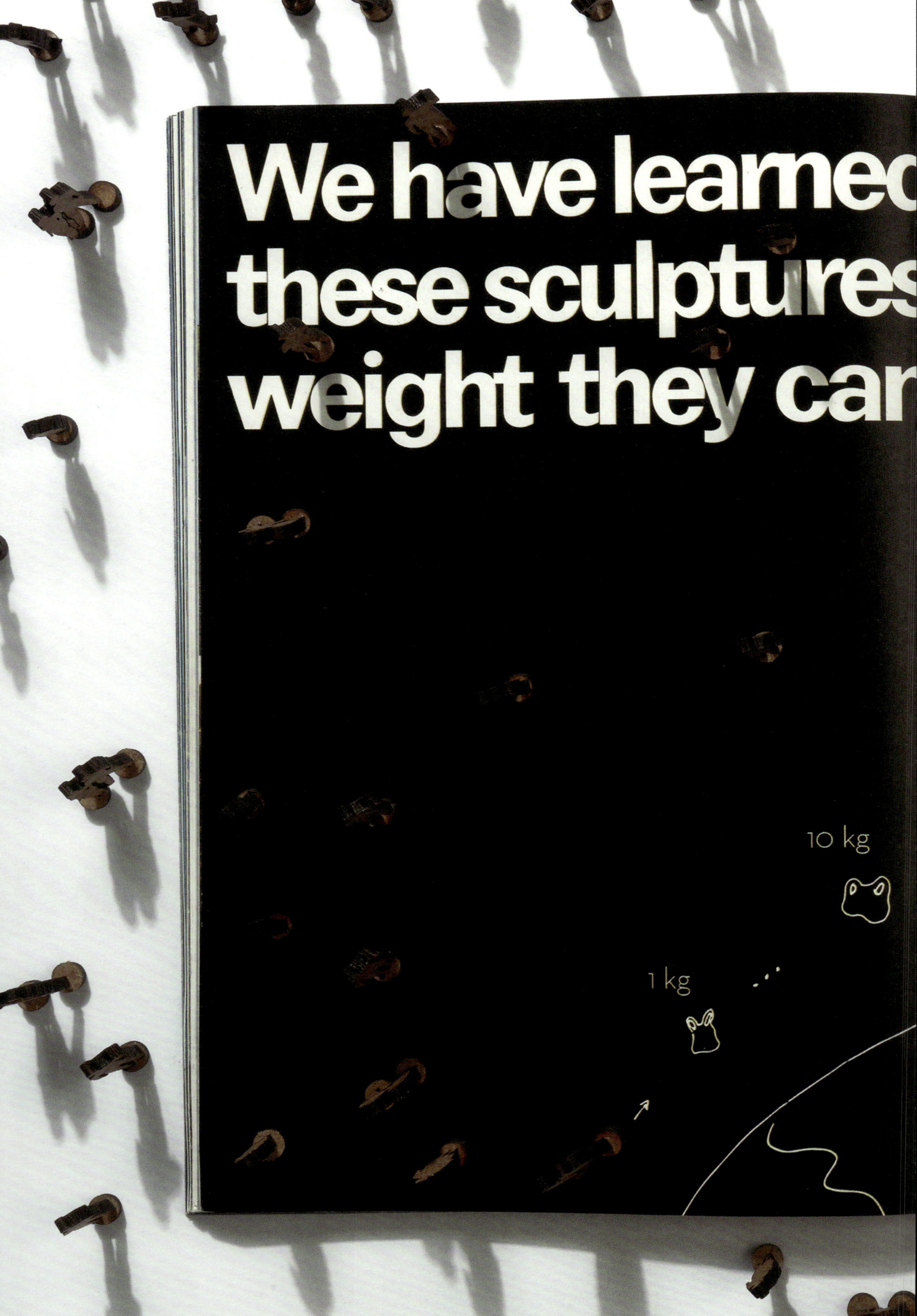
We have learned
these sculptures
weight they can
10 kg
1 kg

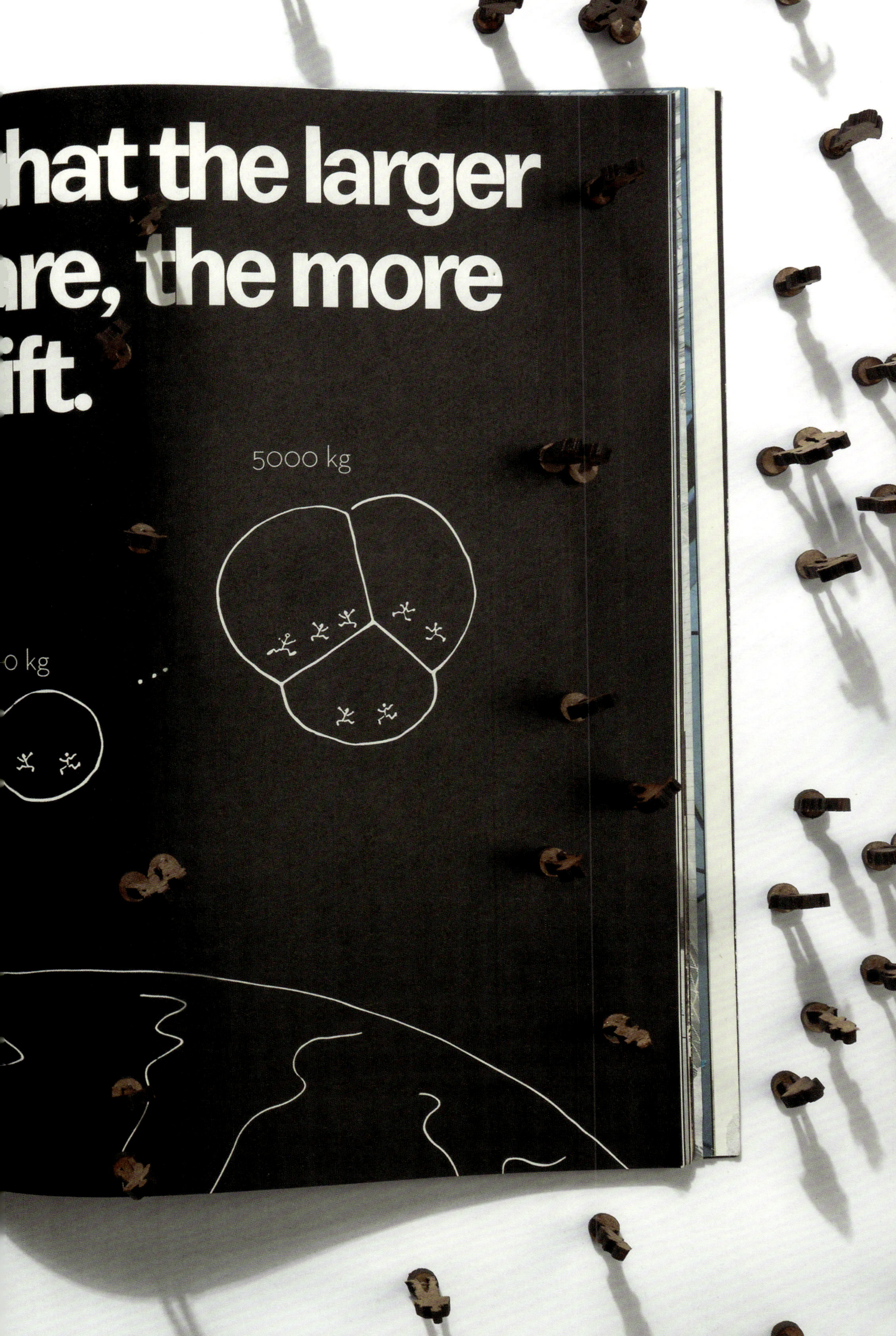
hat the larger
re, the more
ift.
5000 kg
0 kg

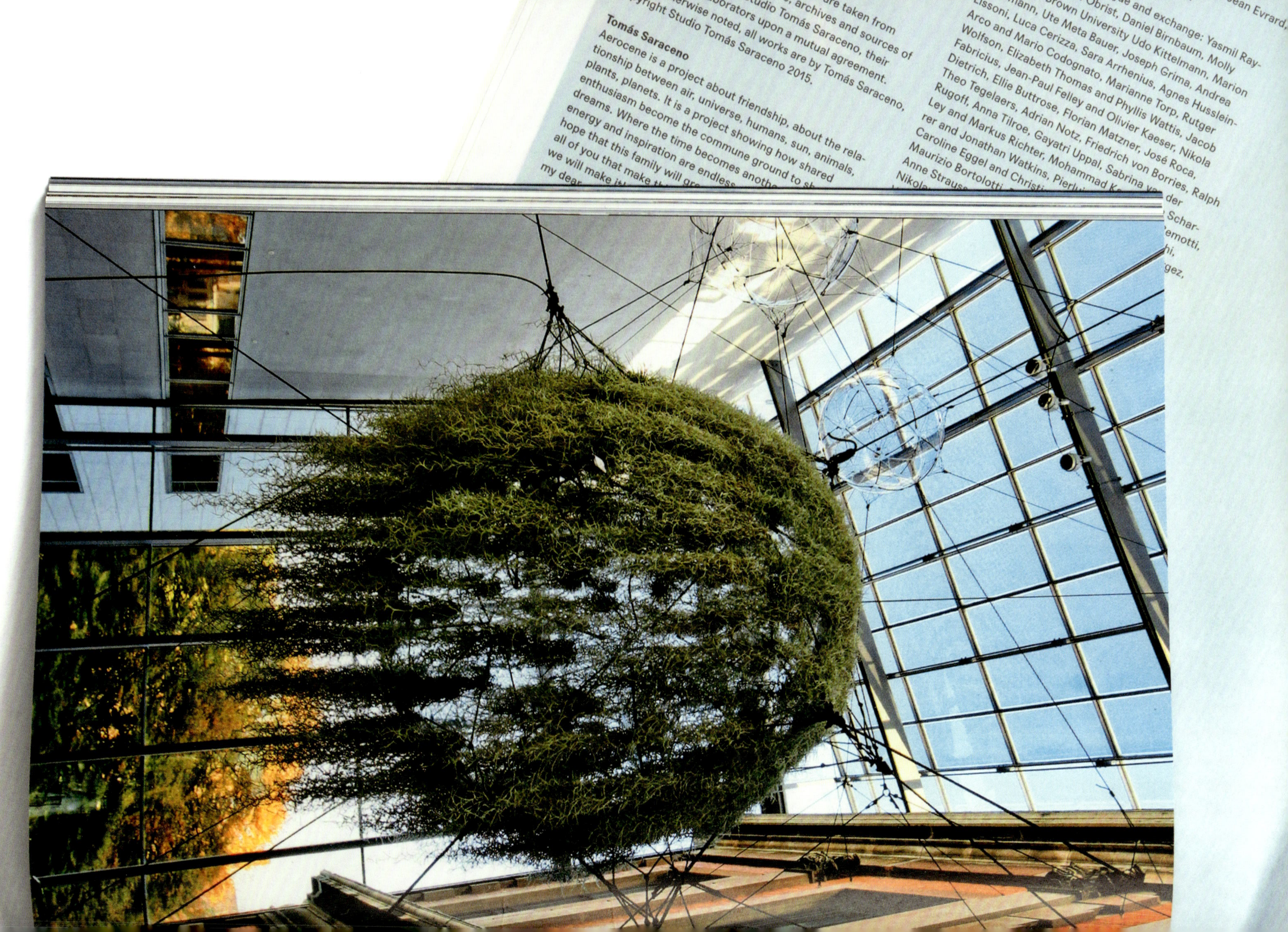

Tomás Saraceno
Aerocene is a project about friendship, about the relationship between air, universe, humans, sun, animals,
plants, planets. It is a project showing how shared
enthusiasm become the commune ground to sh…
dreams. Where the time becomes anothe…
energy and inspiration are endless…
hope that this family will gre…
all of you that make th…
we will make it!…
my dear…

… gue and exchange: Yasmil Ray-
… Obrist, Daniel Birnbaum, Molly
… mann, Ute Meta Bauer, Joseph Grima, Andrea
… Brown University Udo Kittelmann, Marion
Lissoni, Luca Cerizza, Sara Arrhenius, Agnes Husslein-
Arco and Mario Codognato, Marianne Torp, Rutger
Wolfson, Elizabeth Thomas and Phyllis Wattis, Jacob
Fabricius, Jean-Paul Felley and Olivier Kaeser, Nikola
Dietrich, Ellie Buttrose, Florian Matzner, José Roca,
Theo Tegelaers, Adrian Notz, Friedrich von Borries, Ralph
Rugoff, Anna Tilroe, Gayatri Uppal, Sabrina … der
Ley and Markus Richter, Mohammad K…
rer and Jonathan Watkins, Pierlu…
Caroline Eggel and Christi…
Maurizio Bortolotti…
Anne Strauss…
Nikola…

So we learned to build gardens in the air.

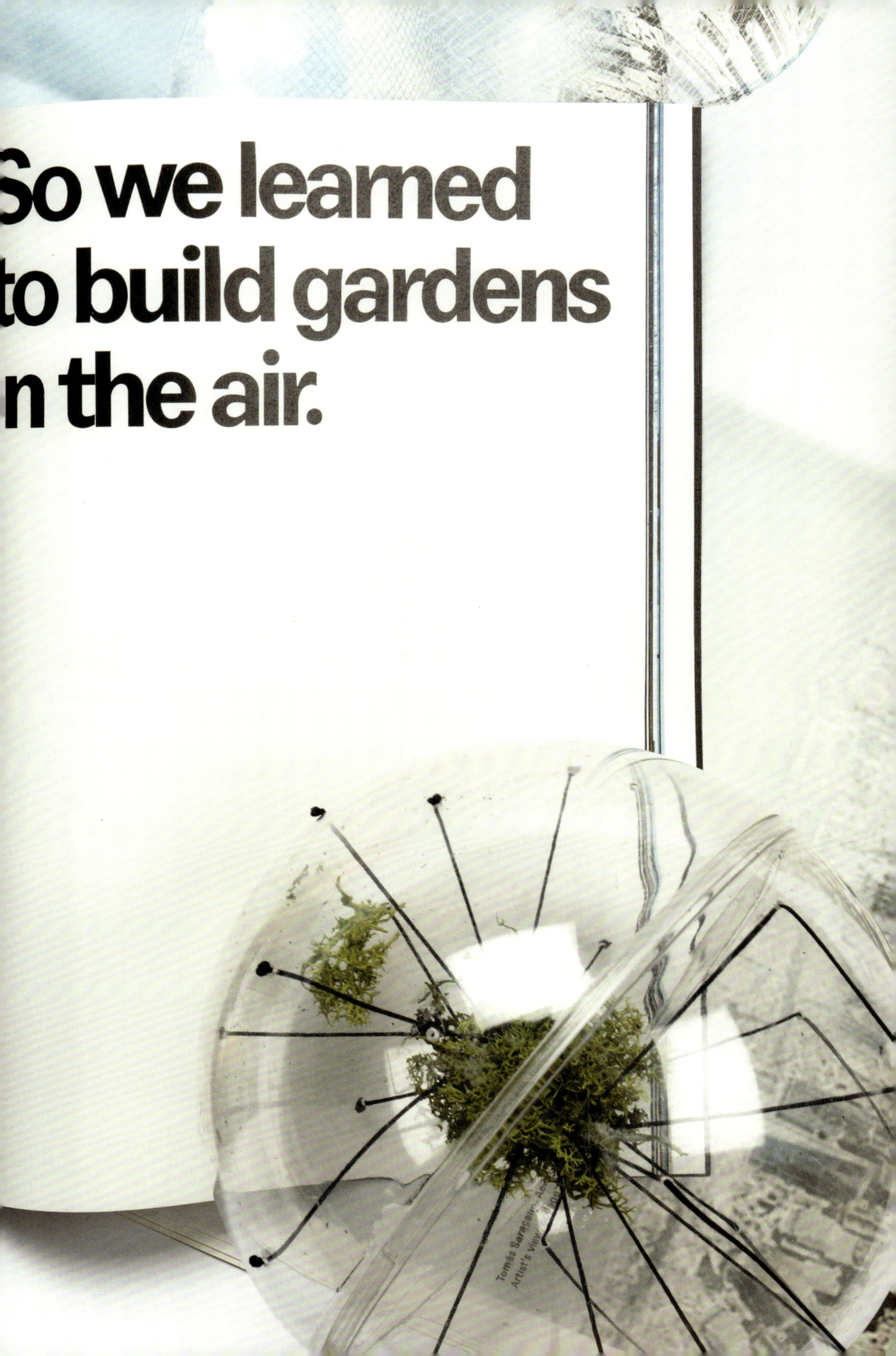

Could we ever live in the air, in a garden the size of the earth?

WHEN THE FIRST FISH
CRAWLED UP ONTO
THE LAND... I'M SURE
ALL ITS FRIENDS THOUGHT
IT WAS CRAZY
... BUT WHY?
MAYBE THERE IS
ANOTHER LIFE FORM
UP THERE!

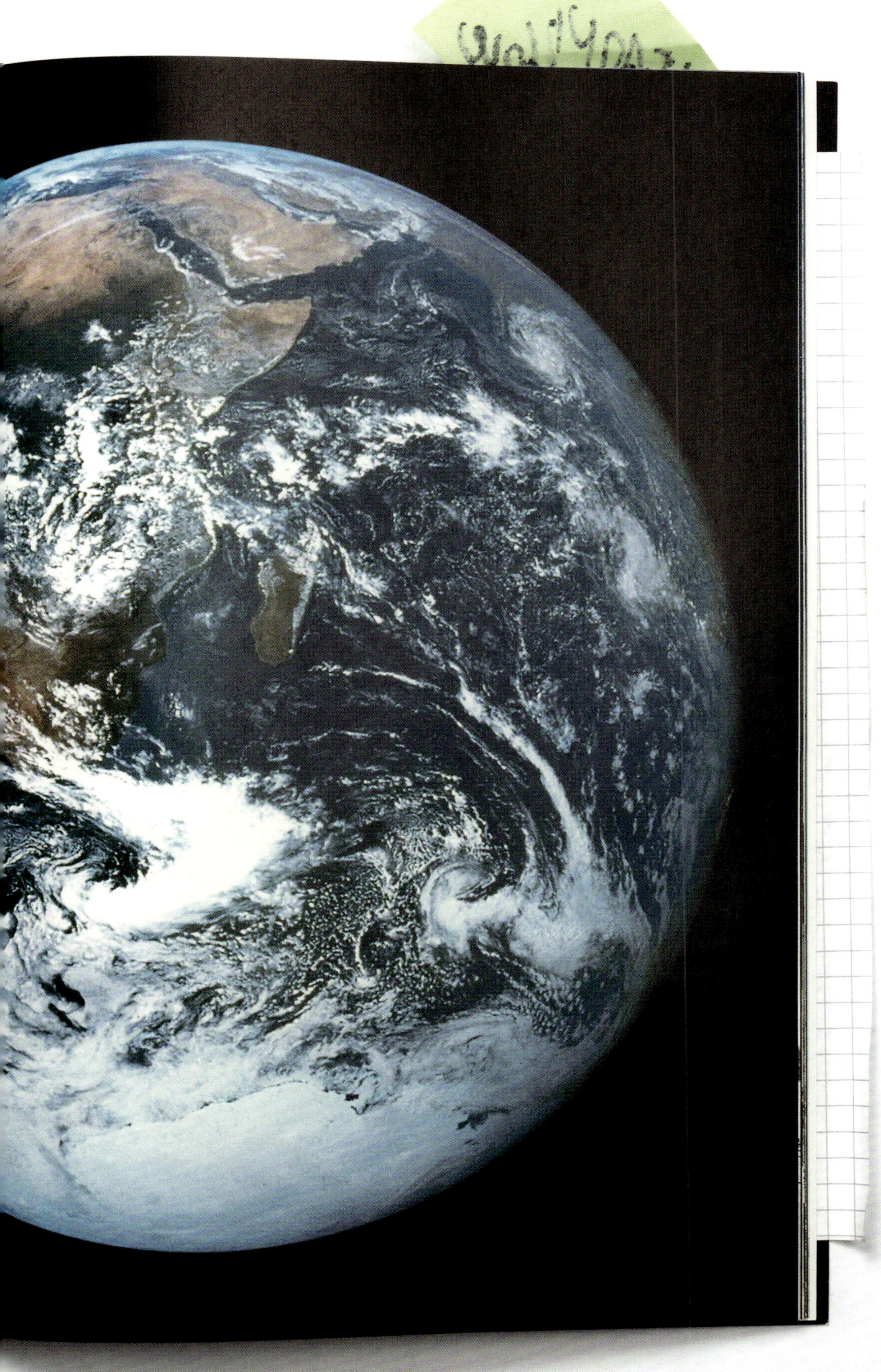

Answering this question is not only a technological challenge.

It is a way of examining freedom of movement between countries and amid political and social constraints,

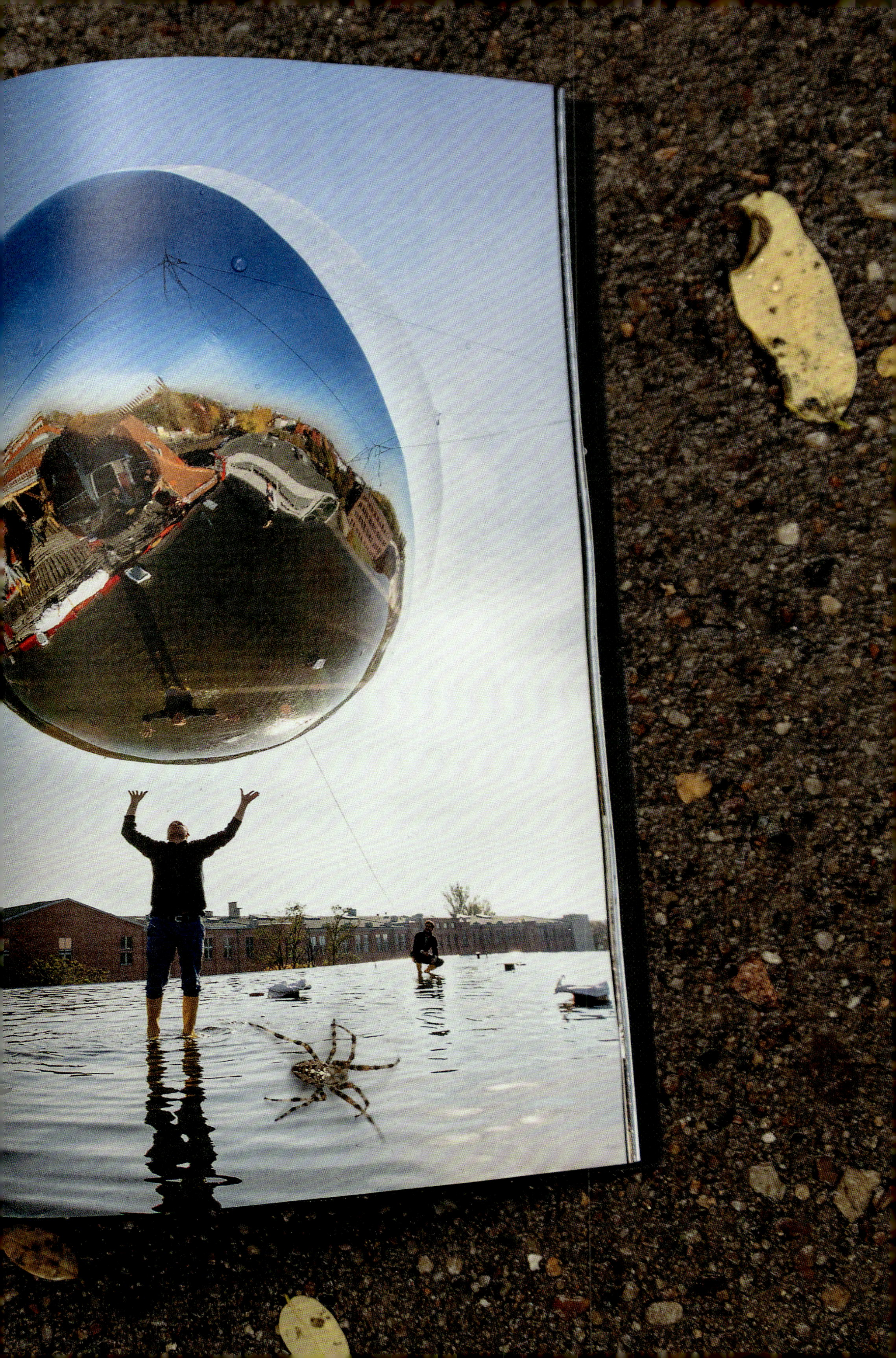

a way of reminding u
relationship with the e

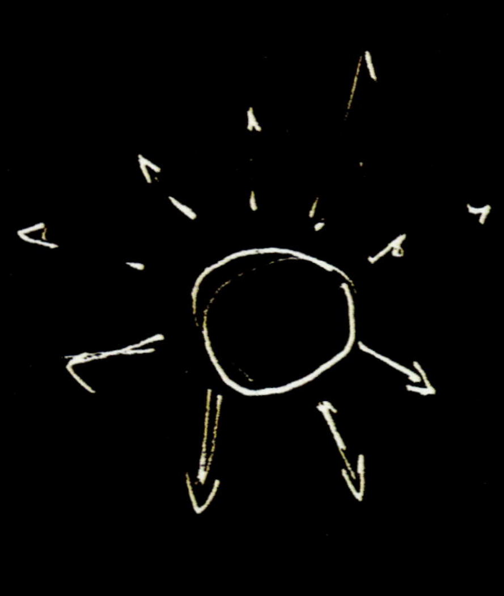

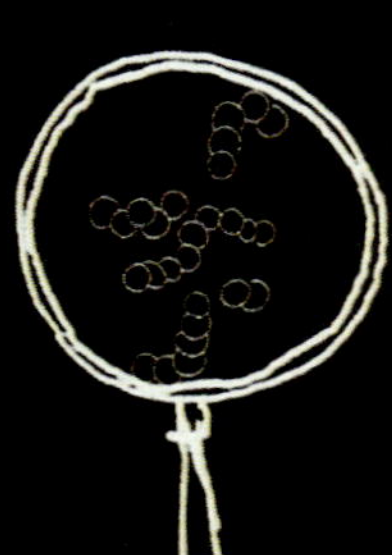

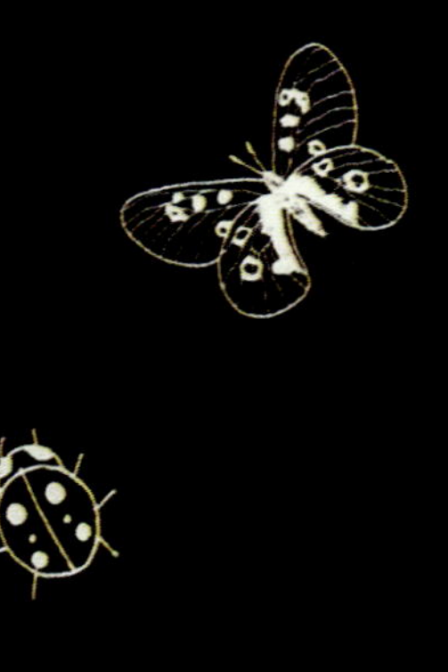

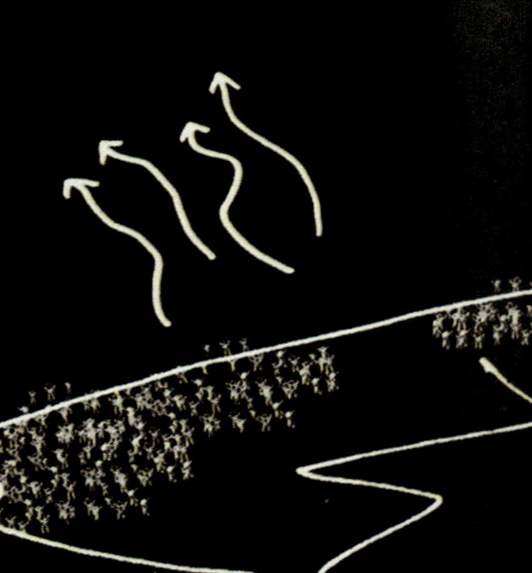

of our symbiotic
th and all its species.

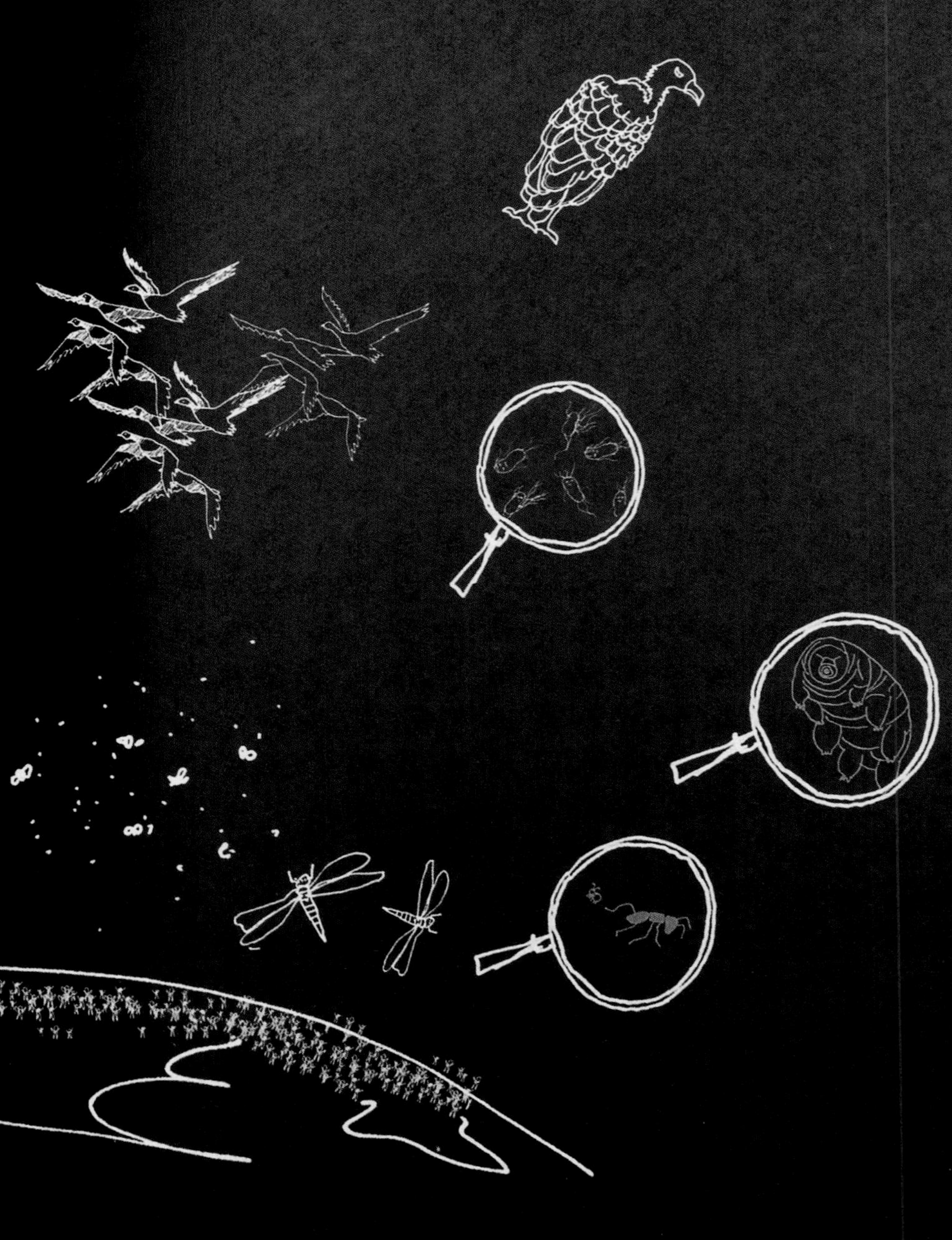

These *Aerocene* spherical sculptures will be able to float us around the world.

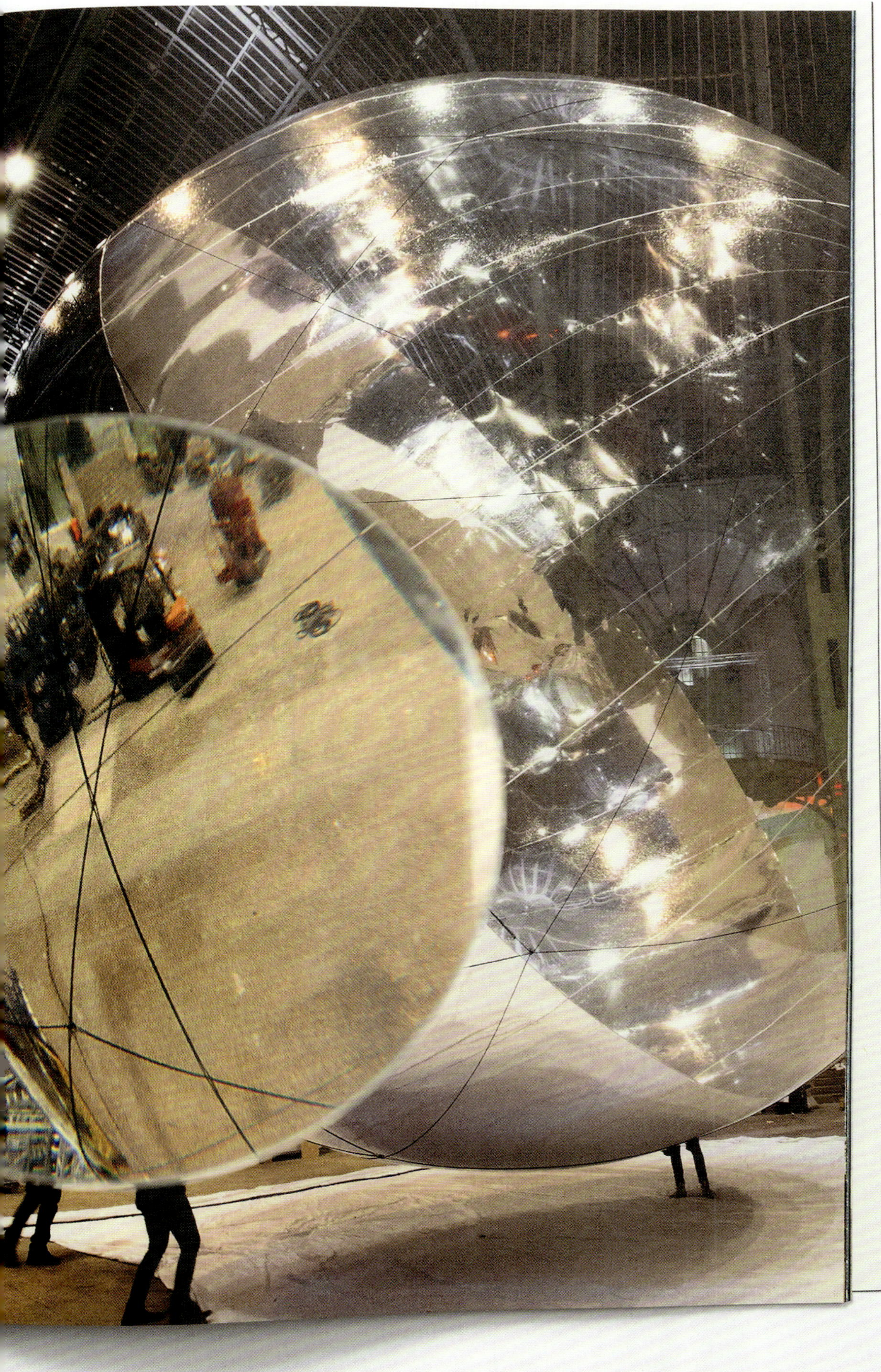

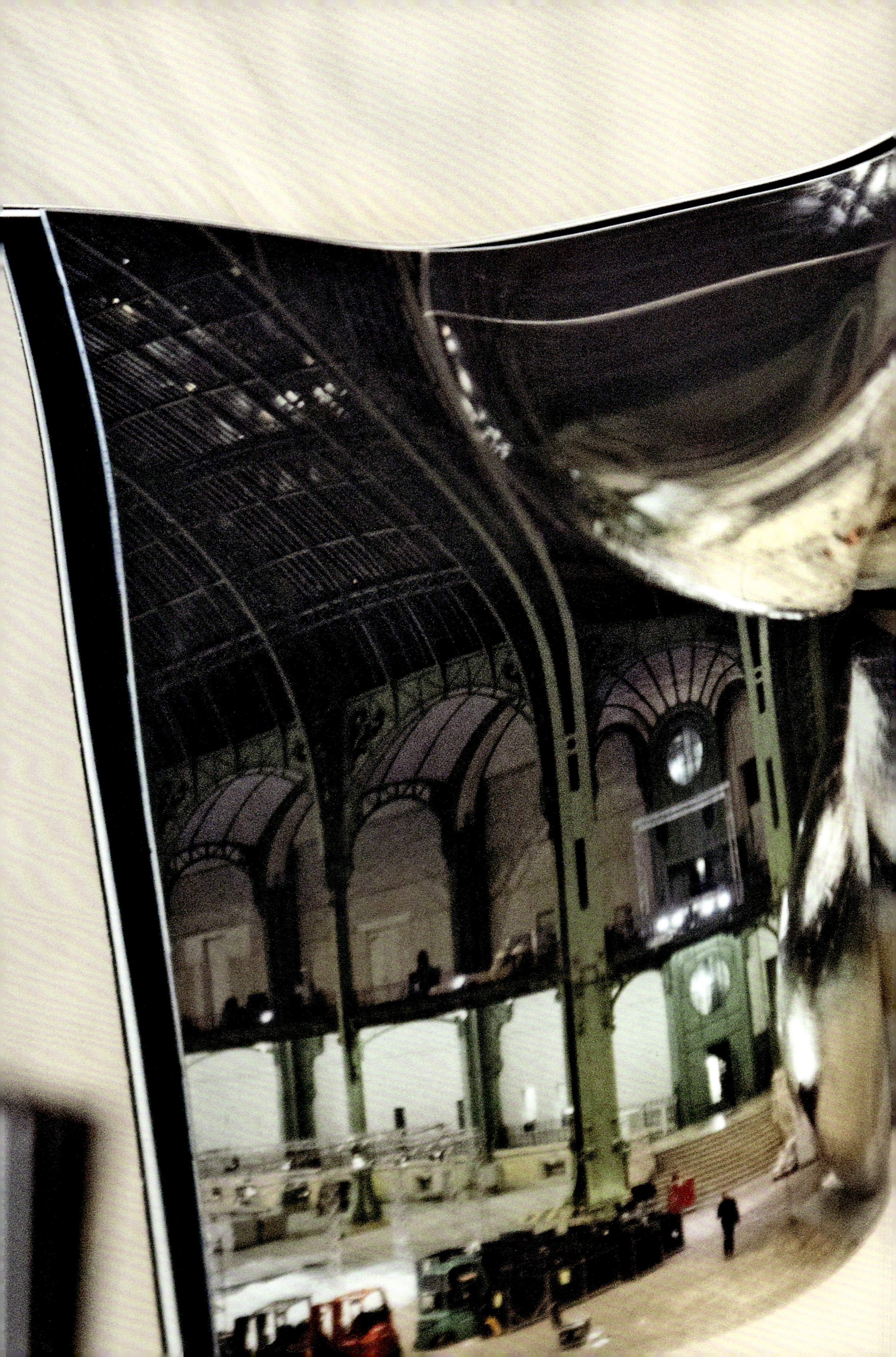

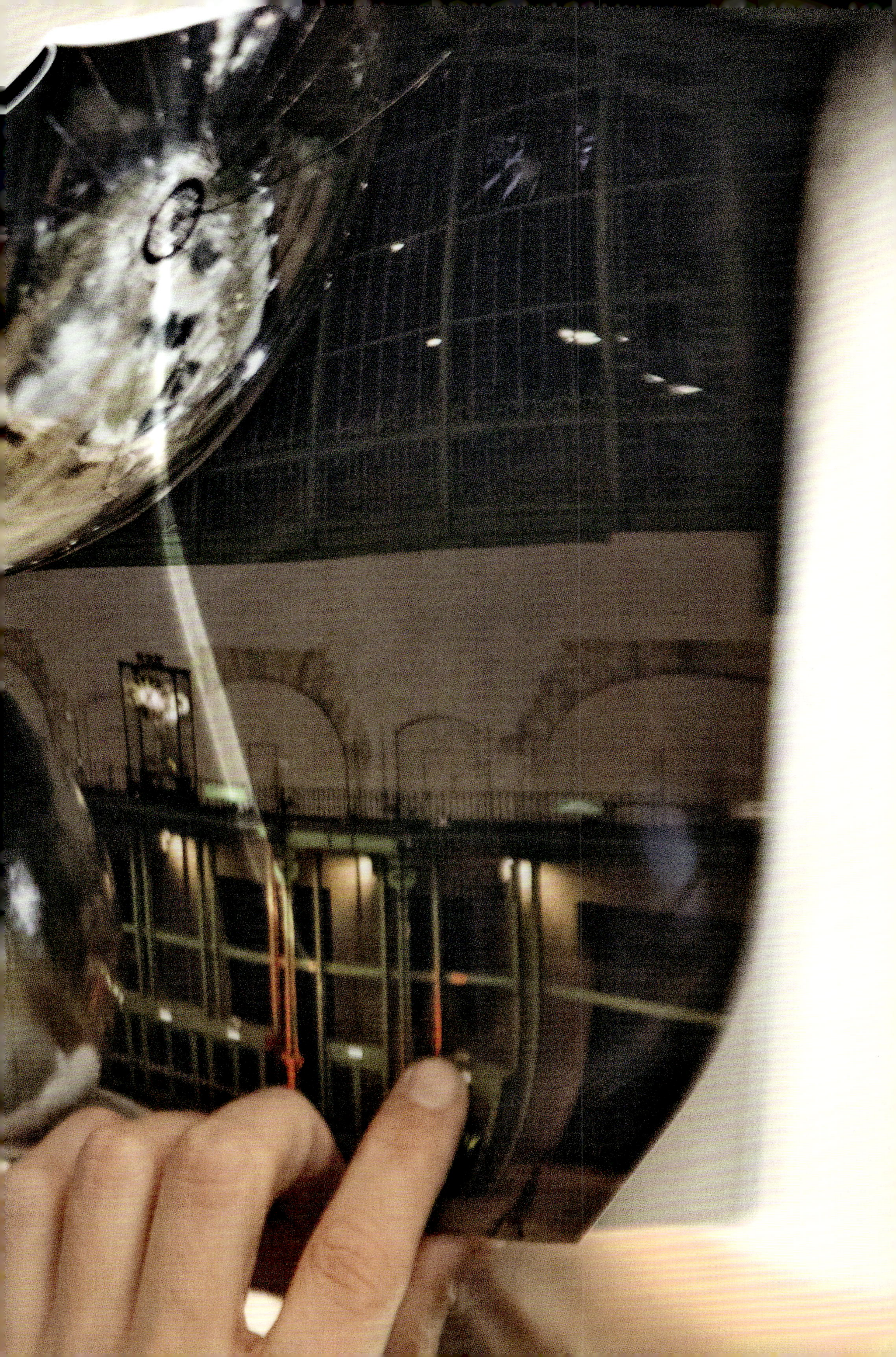

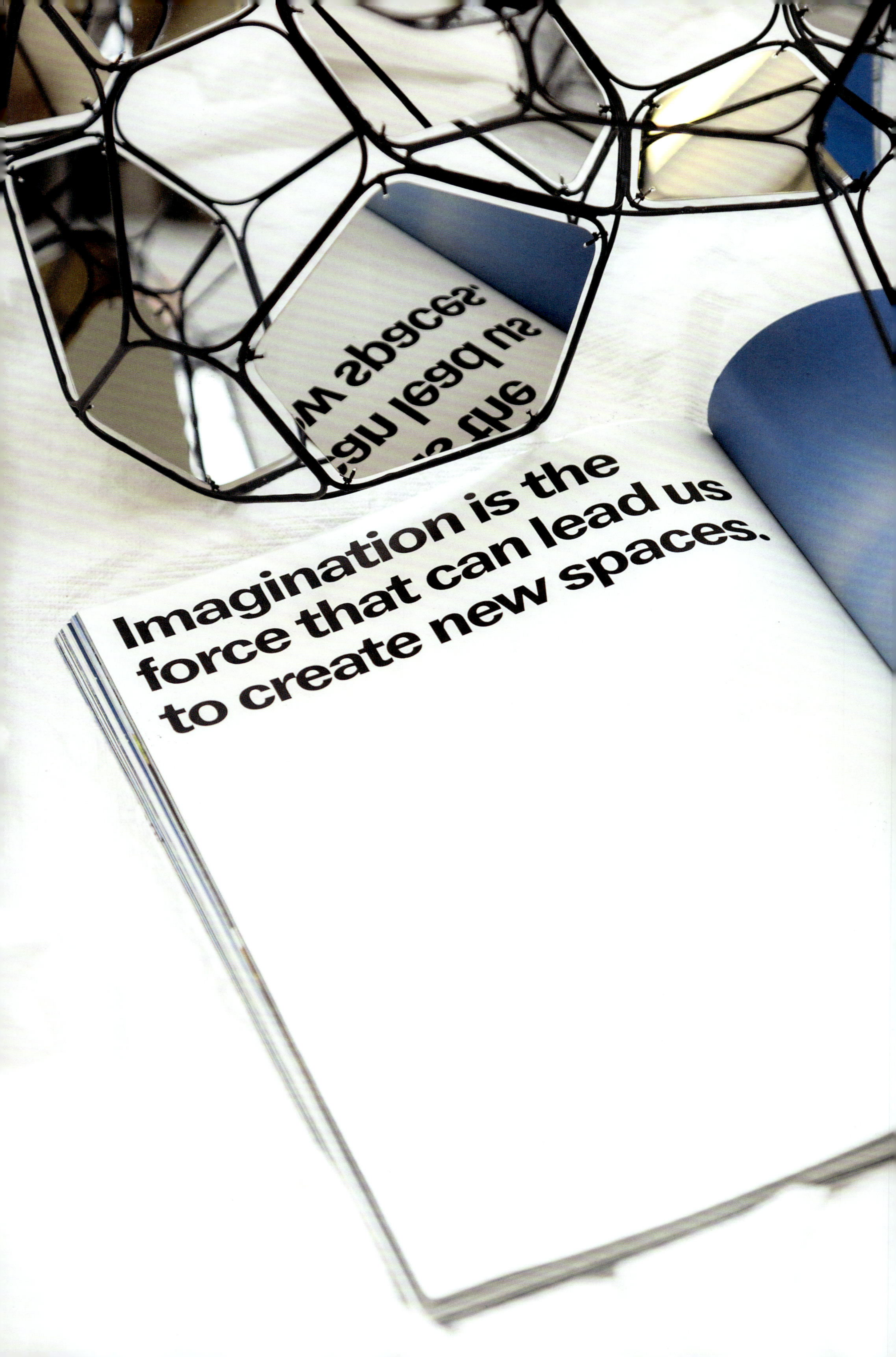

Imagination is the
force that can lead us
to create new spaces.

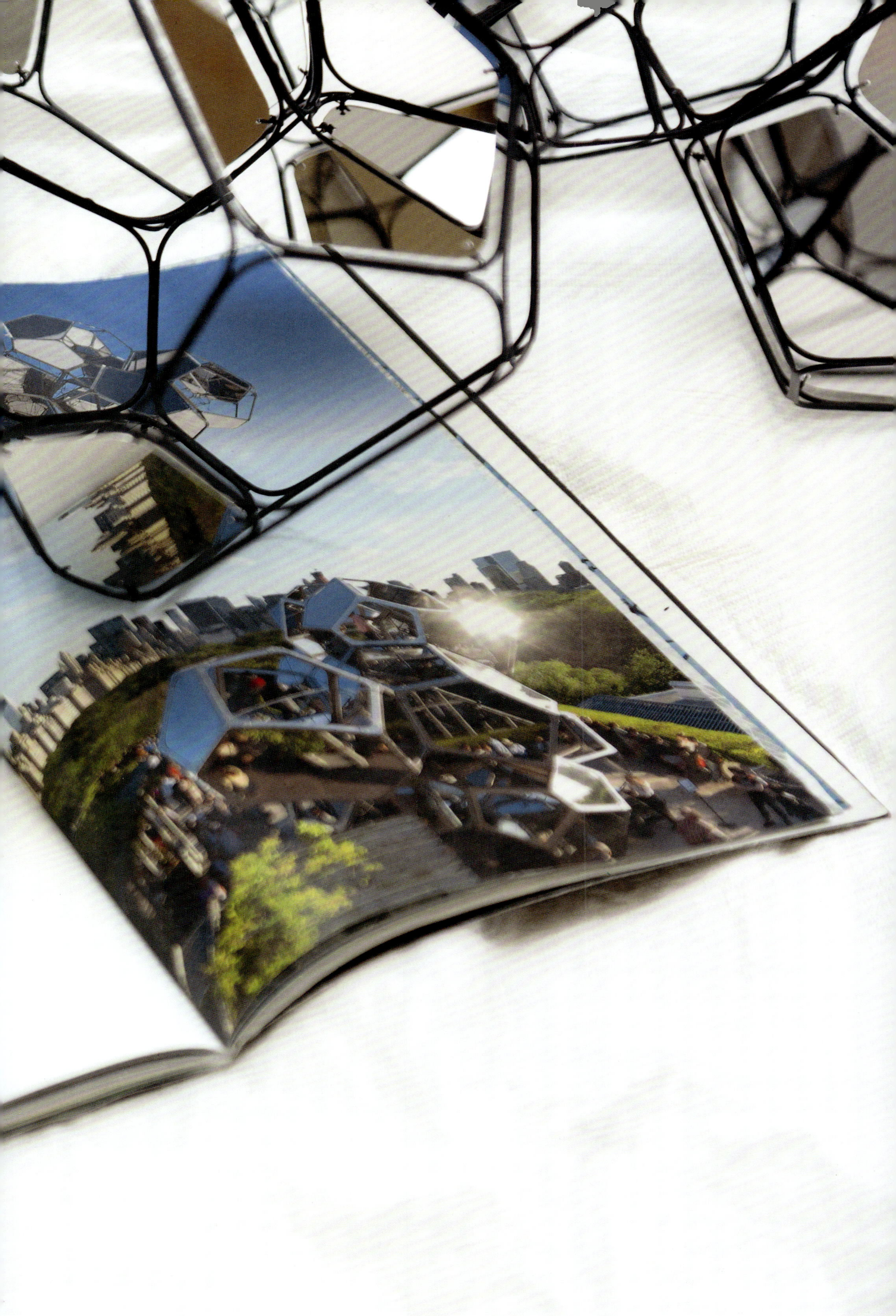

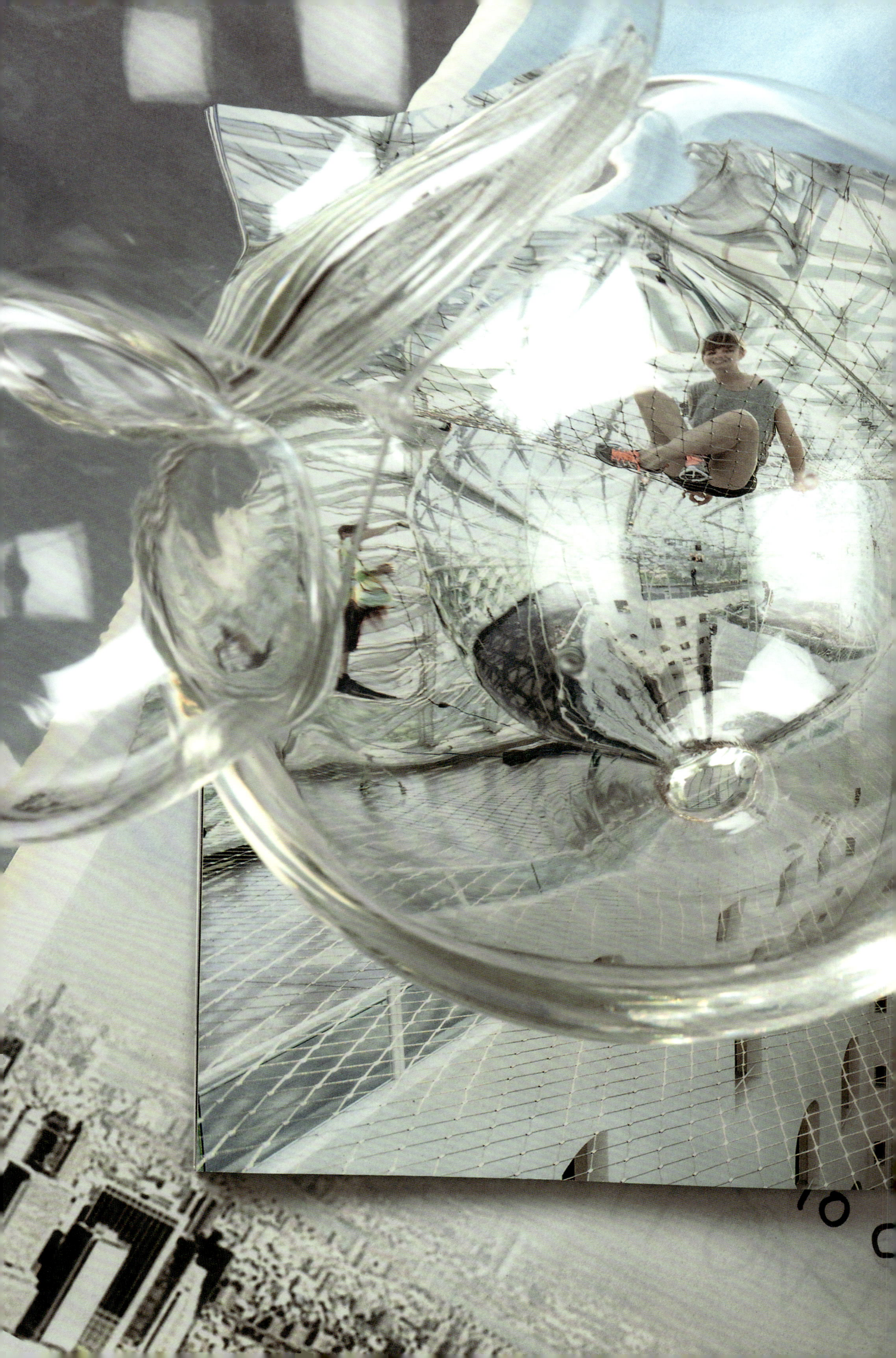

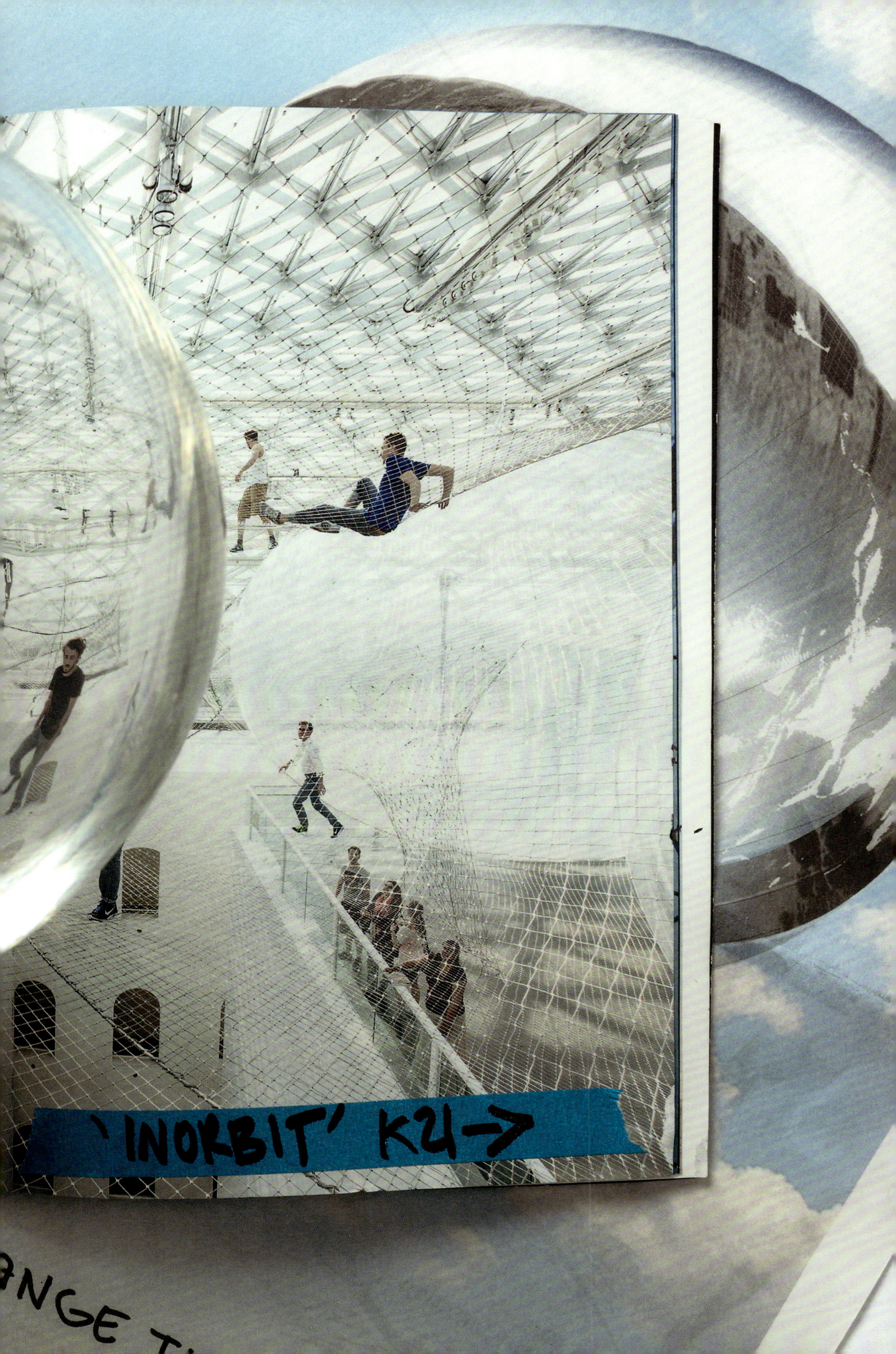
'INORBIT' K2→

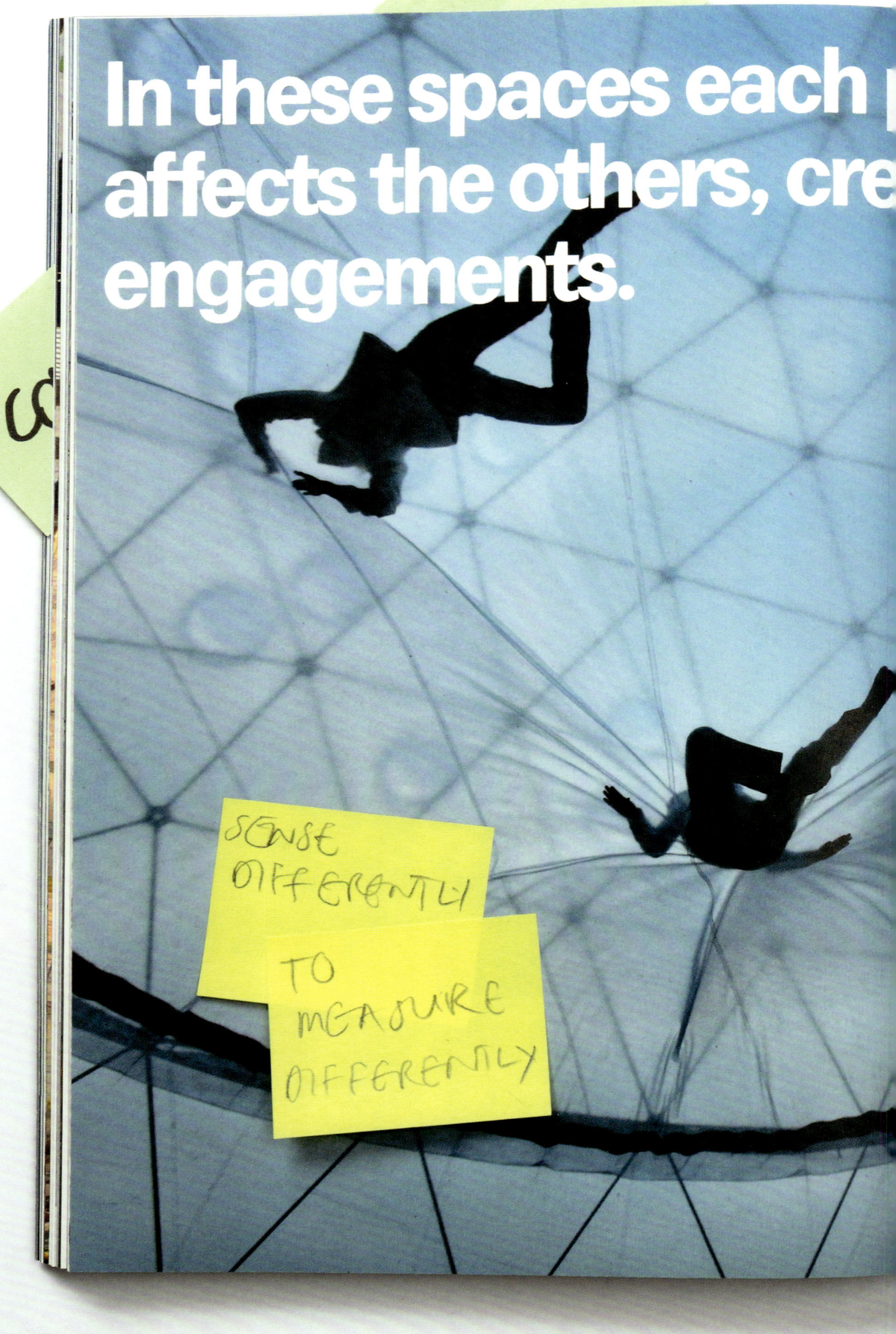
In these spaces each p
affects the others, cre
engagements.
SENSE
DIFFERENTLY
TO
MEASURE
DIFFERENTLY

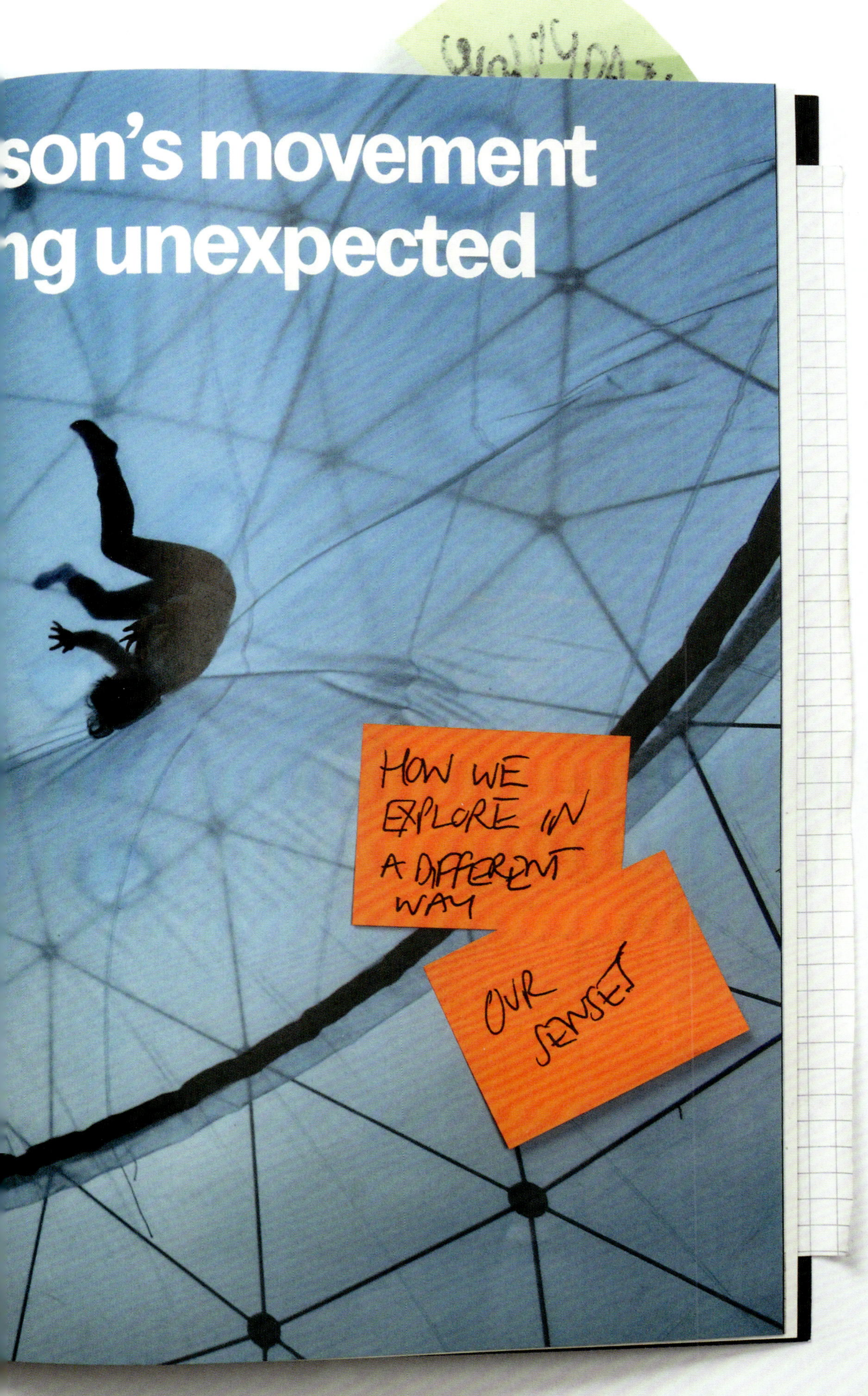
son's movement
ng unexpected
HOW WE
EXPLORE IN
A DIFFERENT
WAY
OUR SENSES

The Anthropocene m
July 16, 1945, at Whit
when the first atomic

As a result of the exp
particles spread all o
years later, on Noven
same location, we w
in the air, only with th
and without burning
flight on record.

have started on
Sands, New Mexico,
bomb was detonated.

osion, radioactive
the earth. Seventy
er 8, 2015, in the
e able to lift a person
power of the sun
any fuel. The longest

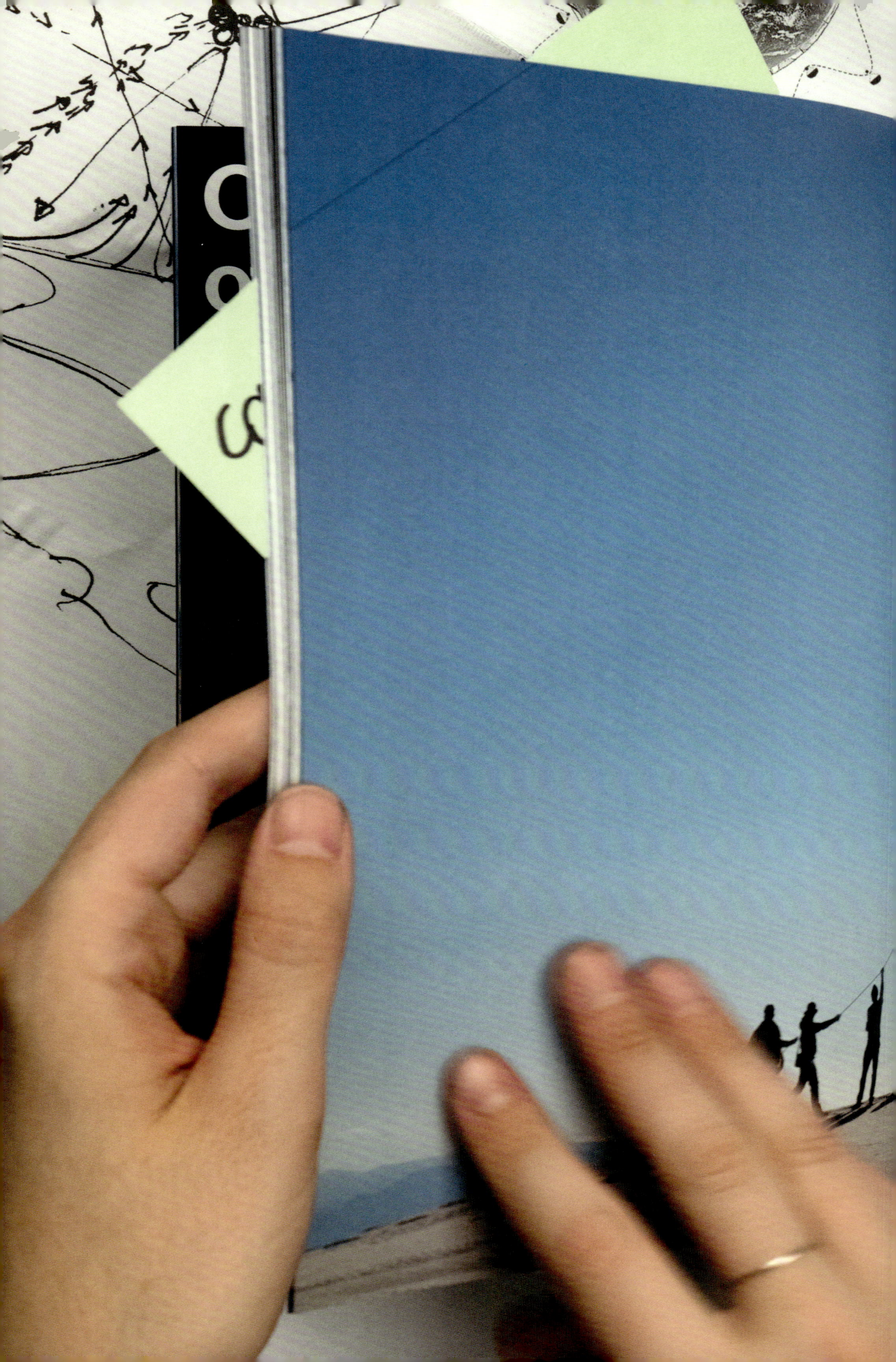

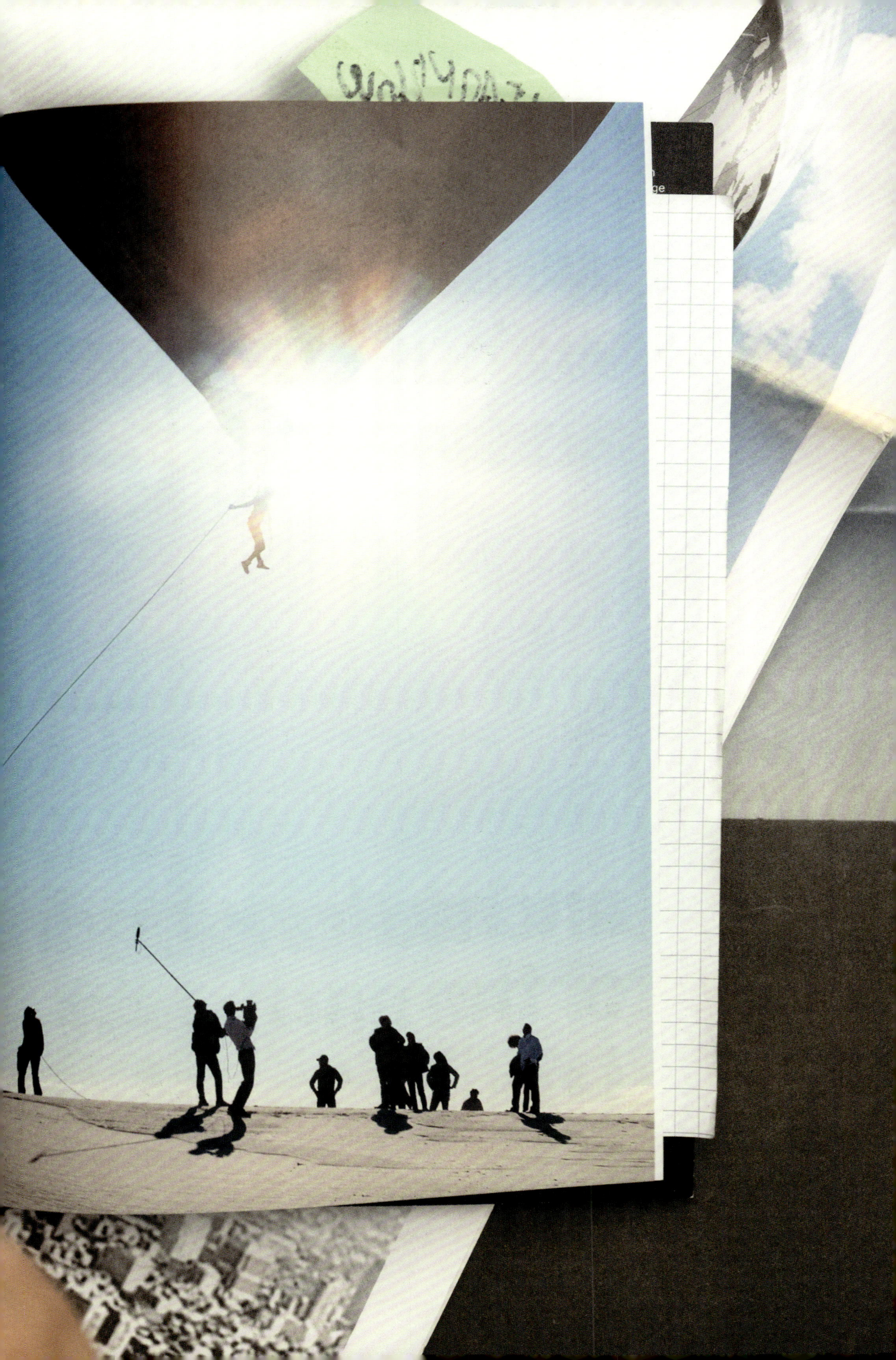

As the sun rose on t
we also rose, silentl
without explosions
and we felt as if gra

and no longer drew
of the earth but
up into the u

horizon,
... slowly ...
...
y were inverted,

us to the center

niverse.

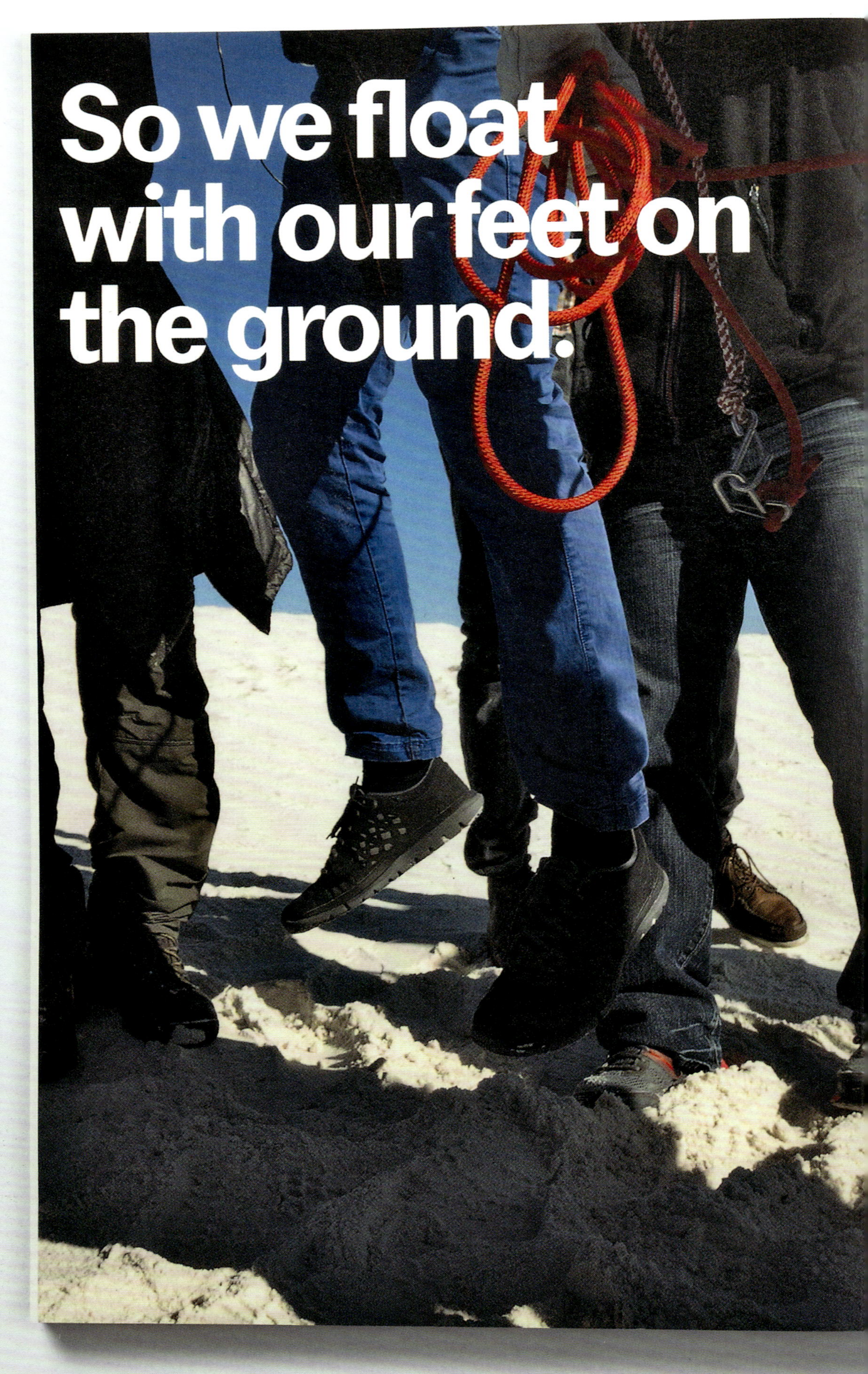

So we float
with our feet on
the ground.

The Aerocene Foundation is a non-profit organisation devoted to community building, scientific research, artistic experience, and education, initiated by artist Tomás Saraceno. Its activities manifest, among other things, in the testing and dissemination of solar sculptures that float without any need for fuel or for rare gases. The Foundation works with artists, thinkers, scientists, researchers, balloonists, technologists, humanitarian workers, and visionaries to increase public awareness of global resource circulation, and reactivate a common imaginary towards new symbiotic relationships with the earth. We are very honoured to work with all these brilliant people around the world: aerocene.org/contributors

The Aerocene Foundation's primary collaborators and supporters are the Center for Art, Science & Technology (CAST) and Earth, Atmospheric and Planetary Science Department – EAPS at the Massachusetts Institute of Technology (MIT), CNES (French National Space Agency), CCK Argentina, Public Lab, The Goethe Institute, Radioamateur, Freifunk, and IAK architecture-related Art Institute at Technische Universität Braunschweig, Red Cross Red Crescent, TBA21, among others. Anyone is invited to share, collaborate, and perform actions in the communal creation and development of the new Aerocene age.

Sincere thank you to thinkers, writers, researchers and advisers: Peter Adey, Barbara Bulc, Pierre Chabard, Nigel Clark, Heather Davis, Sasha Engelmann, Juan Enriquez, Glenn Flierl, Boris Groys, Harriet Hawkins, Tom Hill, Samuel Hertz, Eva Horn, Sir Brian Hoskins, Ludovica Illari, Tim Ingold, Anne Jungblut, Michael Kezirian, Sanford Kwinter, Derek McCormack, Bill McKenna, Olivier Michelon, Kiel Moe, Oliver Morton, Timothy Morton, Hans Ulrich Obrist, Andreas Philippo-pouls-Mihalopoulos, Nicholas Shapiro, Bronislaw Szerszynski, Jol Thomson, Holger Thüs, Etienne Turpin, Philip Ursprung, Leila Wheatley. Special thanks to the designers Michael Heimann and Hendrik Schwantes.

Aerocene has been presented in the following exhibitions: *Aerosolar: Space Without Rockets*, Rubin Center for the Visual Arts, El Paso (curated by Rob La Frenais and Nicola Triscott), *Knowing (in) the Anthropocene*, Haus der Kulturen der Welt, Berlin, *163,000 Light Years*, MARCO, Museum for Contemporary Art, Monterrey (curated by Gonzalo Ortega), Exhibition Road residency at

Goethe Institut (Carlo Rizzo, Angela Kaya, supported by Maja Hoffmann, Francesca von Habsburg and Nicoletta Fiorucci) *Aerosolar Journeys*, Wilhelm-Hack Museum, Ludwigshafen (curated by René Zechlin), *The New Inflatable Moment*, Boston Society of Architects (curated by Mary E. Hale AIA and Katarzyna Balug), *Aerosolar Journeys*, Museum Haus Konstruktiv, Zürich (curated by Sabine Schaschl), *Our Interplanetary Bodies*, Asia Culture Centre, Gwangju (curated by Sung Won Kim) and taken part in: Solutions COP21, Paris (curated by Artists 4 Climate - Didier Saulnier) and Palais de Tokyo (curated by Rebecca Lamarche-Vadel and Jean de Loisy), Meta.morf at TEKS – Trondheim Electronic Arts Centre, Cappadox Festival, The 1st Antarctica Biennale, Socle du Monde Biennale, Herning (curated by Olivier Varenne) and Seoul Biennale of Architecture and Urbanism (curated by Hyungmin Pai and Alejandro Zaera-Polo).

An extended thanks to those who worked on the presentation of the Aerocene Project during *TED The Future You* held in Vancouver, Canada from April 24–27 2017: Andrea Bagnato, Viola Castellano, Connie Chester, Cara Cotner, Anna Garbuglia, Yelta Köm, Camila Palomino, Pedro Portellano, Irin Siriwattanagul and Kotryna Slapsinskaite. For their work on this publication, thanks to Dario Lagana, Ignas Petronis, Sophie Rzepecky and Raj Sandhu.

The Aerocene Explorer is a tethered-flight starter kit, which enables anyone to launch their own Aerocene solar sculpture and start exploring the skies. A tactile and engaging way of experiencing Aerocene, the Explorer allows participants to take aerial photographs and videos and to collect atmospheric data using non-intrusive, emissions-free scientific exploration tools that measure air quality, temperature, humidity, and pressure. The Aerocene Explorer is currently being tested and developed by a global community of artists, geographers, philosophers, thinkers, speculative scientists, explorers, balloonists, and technologists, and other enthusiasts. Warmest thanks to Cara Cotner, Thomas Krahn, Lisa Lurati, Eleonora Pedretti, Karina Pragnell, Daniel Schulz, Irin Siriwattanagul, Sven Steudte, Bronislaw Szerszynski, Erik Vogler, Melina Wanie and Pablo and Janot Mendler de Suarez from Red Cross Red Crescent, Public Lab (Liz Barry and Nicholas Shapiro), IAK architecture-related Art Institute at Technische Universität Braunschweig

(Alexander Bouchner, Sasha Engelmann and Jol Thomson), Exhibition Road Cultural Group (Carlo Rizzo), Imperial College Advanced Hackspace, California College of the Arts (Joseph Becker), and Néstor Kirchner Cultural Centre.

Aerocene Foundation is also supported by Studio Tomás Saraceno: Duncan Anderson, Mateo Argerich, Lars Behrendt, Fabiola Bierhoff, Ally Bishop, Sascha Boldt, Viola Cafuli, Saverio Cantoni, Viola Castellano, Connie Chester, Filippo Corato, Sonia d'Agrain, Nicolas Drummer, Manie Du Plessis, Luca Girardini, Charles Gonzales, Canice Grant, Peter Otto Haas, Alice Hall, Joshua Hoareau, Anna Holzapfel, Katja Kaiser, Georgi Kazlachev, Christos Kollias, Yelta Köm, Dario Laguna, Tobias Lange, Katre Laura, Dominik Lopes, Lisa Lurati, Claudia Melendez, Pepe Menéndez-Conde, Jillian Meyer, Roland Muehlethaler, Evelyn Murphy, Jörg Niemann, Lea Nikou, Aurelia Nowak, Tania Patritti, Eleonora Pedretti, Martina Pelacchi, Ignas Petronis, Marco Pittaluga, Adrian Porikys, Claudia Rech, Patrick Reddy, Antoine Renard, Sophie Rzepecky, Raj Sandhu, Jazmin Schenone, Martin Schlesier, Daniel Schulz, Aysgul Seyhan, Marjan Sharifi, Sebastian Steinboeck, Judith Strassenberger, Ilka Tödt, Christophe Vaillant, Desirée Valdes, Steef Van Lent, Violette Vanderlinden, Erik Vogler, Filippo Vogliazzo, Philipp Weber, Davide Zucco. For their restless help, the representative galleries: Andersen's Contemporary, Ruth Benzacar, Tanya Bonakdar, Pinksummer Contemporary Art, Esther Schipper.

Image Credits:
All images in *Notes on Aerocene by Tomás Saraceno* unless otherwise stated on the page, are ©Photography Studio Tomás Saraceno and courtesy Aerocene Foundation. The editors and the publisher have made every effort to secure permission to reproduce the images in *Notes on Aerocene by Tomás Saraceno*. We apologize for any inadvert errors or omissions. Please visit museoaerosolar. wordpress.com for further documentation of *Museo Aero Solar*. For more documentation of the Aerocene Foundation please visit: aerocene.org.

Edited and published: Studio Tomás Saraceno, Aerocene Foundation
Design: Heimann + Schwantes
Printing: Druckerei Heenemann

Berlin, 2017

Aerocene is a multi-disciplinary project that proposes a new epoch. In the wake of the debates on the Anthropocene, the project foregrounds the artistic and scientific exploration of environmental issues, and promotes common links between social, mental, and physical ecologies.
A synthesis of art, technology and environmental awareness, Aerocene embodies a vision for fossil- and emissions-free travelling and living in the atmosphere.

Aerocene increases public awareness of global resource circulation, and reactivates a common imaginary towards new ways of co-inhabiting the earth.
Its activities manifest in the development and testing of aerosolar balloons, in the distribution of open-source flying kits (the Aerocene Explorer) and in the organization of exhibitions, discussions, and publications with an ever-growing global community.

aerocene.org

Pages 31–130 feature a visual contribution by Tomás
Saraceno and his team in Berlin. The essay tells the
personal account of the collective project *Aerocene* that he
initiated in 2015. It also hints at the creative process that
drives both the project, its community and the artist's
studio practice. It invites every reader to dream together
of floating on cosmic clouds…

Tim Ingold

On Flight

It is perhaps appropriate that I am writing this essay on board a plane. It is a commercial airliner, on a scheduled flight from London to Chicago. I am flying, so it says in the *High Life* magazine that I find in the seat pocket, courtesy of the company that operates the plane. Yet nothing feels less like flying to me. I am cocooned inside a machine that weighs hundreds of thousands of pounds, strapped to a seat that restrains my movement to a wiggling of the toes, and breathing air that circulates the breath of my fellow passengers while remaining hermetically sealed from the atmosphere outside. I find I have become a fiercely territorial animal, defending every centimeter of my armrest and tray table against the incursions of my surly neighbor and his ever-unravelling newspaper. At least I have a window seat, affording a vision of the earth from below. We are passing over North West England, and down there I suppose there are people leading lives not unlike the one I led until, only an hour or two ago, I boarded the plane. Yet I can have no connection with them, not even as fleeting as the wave that one might hazard to onlookers from a passing train. The bafflement, no doubt, is reciprocated: how often, from my own home, have I watched a plane passing high overhead, its fuselage glinting in the sun and painting the sky with its vapor trail, and marveled that inside such a distant object – so remote, so mysterious – there might be people like me, perhaps enjoying their dinner or, more probably, defending their little patches of seating space? Whence came the strange idea that life could be thus packaged up, encapsulated, and dispatched to points across the surface of the globe?

Don't get me wrong. An airliner is a marvelous thing, an object of beauty, a triumph of the techno-scientific imagination, and a testament to the extraordinary twentieth-century history of aviation – a history that has combined ingenuity, endurance and courage with incendiary violence on a previously unimaginable scale. I am thankful that the plane I am on will get me safely to my destination within hours (else you will not be reading this), where in olden times I would have had to suffer weeks at sea followed by a treacherous journey overland. My argument is not against airliners. It is rather against the idea that airliners can fly, or that people can fly in them. Yes: they get off the ground. And yes: they are propelled through the air. But the same might be said of many other things, from cricket balls to cannon shot, most of which come under the general category of missiles. And after 9/11, we hardly need reminding that the airliner, too, can be a missile. The trajectory of the missile is determined by a compound of the force of gravity and the thrust and direction of propulsion. It may be guided by feedback from a target. But to fly is not to surrender to such mechanical determinations, nor is it to draw an arc from a point of origin to a destination. It is rather to find one's way, and one's being, amidst the currents and circulations of atmospheric air. Flying, in short, is not mechanical; it is existential. Birds fly, because to *be* a bird is at once to be a bird-of-the-air. The same is true of other winged creatures, from flying insects to bats. No doubt it was once true of pterodactyls.

Whether it is or has ever been true of humans, however, is moot. It is often said that human beings cannot fly unaided, simply because – as the wise but supercilious Owl reminded Winnie-the-Pooh, in A. A. Milne's immortal fable – they lack the necessary dorsal muscles. Pooh, it will be recalled, had recourse to a balloon, with which he planned to rise into the air and negotiate with the bees, in the hope of obtaining some of their honey. He thought he could actually become an aerial being, akin to a cloud, though the bees – very much to his discomfiture – thought otherwise. Perhaps the closest most of us come to flying is in our dreams, in which we *become bird,* not as a thing of flesh and feathers but as a composition of air and movement in which the dreamer himself is borne aloft and carried along. Flight is the feeling of air-borne life, untethered. But I wonder whether we might nevertheless fly even without losing our earthly bearings, in quotidian life as much as in our dreams. Sometimes, when walking in a strong wind, and especially on high ground, we feel as if we are flying, and perhaps we are. It is an exhilarating experience. "Around, up, above, what wind-walks!", exclaimed Gerard Manley Hopkins in his poem *Hurrahing in Harvest.* There is no doubt that I feel much closer to the birds, and to the experience of flying, when walking in the hills than when sat on this plane. So why should we say – as we usually do on such occasions – that we are walking and *not* flying? Why cannot we do both at once?

On dreams of flying, see Gaston Bachelard, *Air and Dreams: An Essay on the Imagination of Movement* (trans. E. R. Farrell, C. F. Farrell), Dallas, TK: Dallas Institute Publications, 1988: 65–89.

Gerard Manley Hopkins, *Look Up at the Skies!* (ed. R. Warner), London: Bodley Head, 1972: 27.

Are not our heaving lungs as much in communion with the swirling air as are our plodding feet with the earth? Does not breath follow breath as step follows step?

Maybe we should regard walking as two-legged flying: a way of flying that has yet to take off. Indeed flying in this sense bears some comparison with sailing. While the hull of the vessel skims the waves, its sails catch the wind: it is as much airborne as waterborne. Thus sailing, too, could be the mariner's way of flying. And although the analogy might seem far-fetched, I just wonder whether the same might be said of writing, at least as it was practiced in ages before the advent of the printed word. Medieval scribes often drew parallels between their writing and the passage of a wayfarer through the terrain, and between the letter-line traced by the pen and the path traced by feet. Could writing have been the scribe's way of flying, as walking was the pedestrian's way? Don't forget that the scribe would have used a quill pen, made from a feather that had once graced a bird on the wing. Thanks to this feather, it is now the writer's hand that flies, so as to leave its sinuous trace on the page.

Tim Ingold, *Being Alive: Essays on Movement, Knowledge and Description*, Abingdon: Routledge, 2011: 188.

Perhaps the parallel between writing and flying is even more apparent in the oriental traditions of brush calligraphy, which often took inspiration from the flight of birds and the wispy forms of clouds. Here, the flying brush skims the paper, leaving its traces like passing eddies of wind in the dust of dry ground. The walker's lines, the mariner's lines and the writer's lines, let us say, are all *lines of flight,* and what is characteristic of such lines is not just that they are aerial, but that they escape the determinations of origin and target. They go not from A to B but through the midst of things.

On lines of flight, see Gilles Deleuze, Félix Guattari, *A Thousand Plateaus: Capitalism and Schizophrenia* (trans. B. Massumi), London: Continuum, 2004: 323.

It is no accident that "to flee" and "to fly" are etymologically cognate, and that both conjugate to "flight."

Today, of course, the writer is typically no longer a scribe or a calligrapher but a wordsmith, whose verbal compositions are committed to page or screen by means of a mechanism.

Tim Ingold, *Lines: A Brief History,* Abingdon: Routledge, 2007: 128–9.

Yet we still call the typed or printed document a "manuscript," *as if* its lines were drawn in the flight of the hand. The same wishful anachronism is at work when we speak of the flight of the airliner, or the sailing of its ocean-going counterpart. Just as it is impossible to write – in the original sense of scribing or tracing a line – with a keyboard, so, strictly speaking, it is not possible to fly with the plane or to sail with the ship. The liner's line does indeed go from A to B. The ship, with its propellers, drills through the ocean as though making a hole through which it can pass, much as the airliner – once equipped with propellers but now with jet engines – bores its way through the sky. In one case water, in the other air, is both a medium and a resistance to be overcome, and this is done by using an external power source to induce a turbulence that is foreign to its nature. But the fish in the water and the bird in the air operate quite differently. Their bodies, equipped with fins and wings, are designed to move not *against* the medium but *with* it, coupling their own energies with its fluid dynamics. Water for the fish and air for the bird is not a homogeneous mass through which one has relentlessly to drill, as does the tunneler through solid rock, but a highly differentiated texture, woven by materials in motion to create the eddies and thermals that denizens of the ocean and the sky can both harness and inflect to their advantage.

Looking out from my passenger window I can see something of this texture in the formations of clouds that currently blanket the earth. It is otherwise invisible to us. Yet birds can feel it, and so I suppose can glider pilots and balloonists. I regret that I have never flown in either a glider or a balloon. Nor have I ever dropped to earth in a parachute, flown a microlight or indulged in the sport of skydiving. I therefore have little authority to write on these matters, and must rely on the testimony of others. One account comes from the artist Peter Lanyon, who took up gliding in 1959 as a way to enrich his previous practice of landscape painting. Lanyon had this to say of one of his most extraordinary works, *Thermal,* painted a year later. "The air is a very definite world of activity as complex and demanding as the sea. The thermal itself is a current of hot air rising and eventually condensing into cloud. It is invisible and can only be apprehended by an instrument such as a glider. The basic source of all soaring flight is the thermal." This is a quotation from the Tate Gallery display caption. But the painting not only

See http://www.tate.org.uk/art/artworks/lanyon-thermal-t00375, accessed 29th February 2016.

references gliding. It also describes the flight of seabirds as they negotiate the cliffs. They too must ride the complex currents that the wind sets up as it scours the rock-face. Or it could reference the predatory hawk which, having risen on the upward current, must strain muscle and sinew to hold a position directly above a location on the ground, preparing to swoop on unsuspecting prey. At last relaxing, it soars away on the wind. What looks like stillness for us is motion for the hawk, and conversely, what we see as motion is the hawk's way of staying still.

It is the same for balloonists who, up aloft, report an overwhelming sense of stillness. Precisely because the craft is moving with and not against the wind, it is as though one were becalmed. Down below, people might be holding on to their hats, but up above, all is quiet. Below, the wind wants to tear you away; above, you float in it. Stillness, in short, is the perfect condition of movement, when all its elements are in harmony. We alight here on a profound truth, first enunciated by the Graeco-Sicilian philosopher Empedocles in the fifth century BC. The cosmos, according to Empedocles, is formed through the perpetual dialogue of two opposed principles, which he named Love and Strife. Love, in its purest form, is spherical. Within the sphere, all the elements are in accord with one another; only at its surrounding surface does strife come into play. But it is Strife that – by tearing the elements apart, mixing them and forming new combinations thereof – gives rise to all the material phenomena that we observe around us. In his time, Empedocles appealed to mythology to give body to his principles, in the figures of Aphrodite and Ares, deities respectively of Love and of Strife. Had he however been alive in the pioneering days of balloon flight, in the eighteenth and nineteenth centuries, he might well have seen in the balloon the perfect embodiment of Love, and in the force of the wind that would fain pull it from its moorings the epitome of Strife. But on a smaller scale, one has only to attend to the lowly soap bubble, all stillness and harmony within but bounded by the forces of surface tension in the liquid medium. Eventually and inevitably, strife prevails, the bubble bursts: its liquid falls to earth and its inner breath vanishes into air.

Here I am on board an airliner, reflecting on stillness! It is paradoxical. I may be sitting perfectly still, with my seat-belt properly fastened in case of unexpected turbulence – those disconcerting moments when powerful

atmospheric forces shake our confidence in the homogeneity of the medium –
but I am chronically restless. I have an urge to move my limbs but cannot,
and feel the stillness as a restraint. This is Strife, not Love. I want to get from
London to Chicago as quickly as possible, and the time it takes is a measure
of my impatience. Ideally, it should take no time at all. But then I soothe my
restless mind with thoughts of floating bubbles, of dandelion clocks wafting
on a summer's day, of stray particles of dust lit by sunbeams. Pictures of all of
these, and more, may be found in the advertising pages of *High Life* magazine,
which promise a utopia of peace and relaxation at journey's end – conditional,
of course, on the payment of large sums of money. These pictures only rein-
force the sense of inaccessibility, yet they appeal precisely because they res-
onate with real experience and pleasing memories. Yes: my attention too has,
on occasion, wandered with soap bubbles and dandelion clocks, and in those
moments I have felt the sense of stillness, and of harmony, that Empedocles
described as Love. But then, this stillness is not an absence of movement.
Absolute immobility would be tantamount to death. A living body has to
breathe, its heart has to beat; blood has to circulate in its veins. We experience
stillness when these bodily rhythms are in tune with the movements around
us. That is why the hawk is still as it soars on the thermal, why fish are still as
they dart about in the water, why the balloon is still as it drifts wherever the
wind will take it, and why I am still as my attention remains rapt in the floating
bubble – until it bursts.

These are the stillnesses of being alive, of harmonic sound rather than
enforced silence. They are stillnesses that are held in movement, rather than
striving against it. In his prose poem *On the Nature of Things*, composed around
50 BC, the Roman author Lucretius put this in a nutshell:

> Herein wonder not
>
> how 'tis that, while the seeds of things are all
>
> Moving forever, the sum yet seems to stand
>
> Supremely still.

Titus Lucretius Carus, *On the Nature of Things* [*De Rerum Natura*] (trans. W. E. Leonard), New York: Dutton, 1921: 38.

Lucretius was a great admirer of Empedocles, and even used Empedocles's poem, *On Nature,* as a model for his own exposition. But for Lucretius the cosmos, in its purest or most pristine form, was not spherical but rectilinear. It was made up of innumerable atoms, perpetually raining down in parallel through the infinitude of space. Yet they have only to swerve a little in their course to collide with one another, and it is in the cascading of these collisions that a world is formed, consisting of endless permutations and combinations of matter. But we see the forms and not the flow, Lucretius argued: the world to us seems still even though it is entirely suspended in movement. Now listen to the philosopher Henri Bergson, writing a couple of millennia later, in the early twentieth century:

> Like eddies of dust raised by the wind as it passes, the living turn upon themselves, borne up by the great blast of life. They are therefore relatively stable, and counterfeit immobility so well that we treat each of them as a thing rather than as a progress, forgetting that the very permanence of their form is only the outline of a movement.
>
> Henri Bergson, *Creative Evolution* (trans. A. Mitchell), New York: Henry Holt, 1911: 128.

Bergson is with Lucretius in thinking that life in general is given in movement, and moreover in his conviction that for there to be particular living things it is necessary for this movement to veer from a course that would otherwise be absolutely straight. But unlike Lucretius, he saw the movement as going ever upwards, not downwards. Bergson was writing at a time when balloon flight was in its heyday, and it is quite possible that in writing of the "great blast of life," he had the hot air balloon in mind.

But what of myself, aboard this airliner? I am borne up, to be sure, not however by the blast of life but by the blast of jet engines burning fossil fuel. And my immobility is not so much the outline of a movement as the product of its constriction. I am cocooned in a blast of death, projected towards my destination in a guided missile, while I dream of bubbles and dandelion clocks … until rudely awakened by the thud of wheels on tarmac. My plane has landed. I stagger off to join an immigration queue. Maybe, once I am out of the terminal and back into the open air, I can begin to fly!

Timothy Morton

Floating as Ecological Action

An environment is a necessarily dynamic, unstable thing that surrounds and penetrates us. We are part of it, and we exceed it. We are it, and we aren't it. It entangles us in a loop, but this doesn't mean that nothing can happen.

Our idea of "part of" and our idea of "entangle" usually means "is completely locked into an overarching structure" and "completely bind together." The world of balloons and biospheres and environments and nonhuman beings – the world we have been seeing as separate from us in various ways, and which we have often called Nature (capital N) – is a world of machine-like components moving about, but not acting. Behaving. Being passive.

Humans act. Everything else behaves.

What happens when we start to see ourselves as one of those things "over there" like balloons and bunny rabbits and biospheres? The name for this seeing is Anthropocene. The Anthropocene is the moment at which humans realize that they are a geophysical force on a planetary scale. Unwittingly, despite ourselves, and having nothing to do with our individual thoughts and our individual actions (which are statistically meaningless), *unconsciously* in other words, humans as a species are like the asteroid that wiped out so much life on Earth in the last mass extinction event, sixty-five million years ago. What is disturbing about this new vision is that humans notice that we are not just on one side of the equation – the side that gets to act. We are on the other side as well: we are *behaving*, despite what we want and even despite our specific individual actions. It's like we woke up one day to find that we were holding a knife in our hand and that there is a corpse lying in bed next to us. How on earth did we become murderers? Murder is exactly right – it's not just an analogy, because what global warming, one of the features of the Anthropocene means, is mass extinction, the sixth one on this planet in the four-billion-year history of life on Earth. The human species is the mass extinguisher this time, not a gigantic asteroid. We are the asteroid.

Along with this realization, we wake up to find that this "human" category is real – jellyfish didn't cause mass extinction, humans did – but that there's a lot less of it than we thought. We wake up to realize that "human" means a loose, symbiotic network of human and nonhuman parts. For example, there is so much more non-Tim Morton DNA in Tim Morton, in order for him to exist. Stomach bacteria, mitochondrial DNA – just so much more. The human species is not human-flavored all the way through, it doesn't have the equivalent of "Intel Inside" stickers on every part of itself. It's a whole, but it's not a whole that swallows its parts completely. It's a hyperobject, massively distributed in time and space, consisting of contradictory parts that aren't totally exhausted by it.

The scary thing is finding out we're the asteroid. The not so scary thing is finding out that there's ontologically much *less* of us than we thought. Hyperobjects are gigantic, godlike beings: they have terrible, disturbing powers. But unlike the Neoplatonic Christian god, they can't be omnipresent or omniscient or omnipotent. They are physically huge, but ontologically tiny compared with their manifold parts.

So thinking this thought as if we were discovering some gigantic all-powerful Cthulhu-like being, without humor, as in a horrific rewrite of the Book of Revelation, isn't ecological at all. It's just another version of Neo-platonic Christianity, which in essence is nihilism for the masses. The physical world, according to this view, is an unreal, illusory, impotent reflection of a real, totally transcendental world to which we have no access. Actually existing flowers and clouds aren't important. Triumphal theism, sometimes disguised as materialist atheism, is exactly the ideology of the agricultural mode that resulted in industrial society, which resulted in global warming and mass extinction. Seeing ourselves as insignificant parts of a murderous god whose behavior we can only witness with awe and horror is a huge part of the problem.

If we're not acting, something else must be. We must be parts of the gigantic machine that is the true actor. Or, acting is a pathetic anthropocentric illusion and everything is automated behavior. Or, we are acting, we must seize control of the moment and make decisive incisions in the inert, passive medium of everything nonhuman. For example, we could master Earth "in a better way" through geoengineering.

Can you see how these sorts of thought are symptoms of our clinging to a rigid binary of *acting* versus *behaving, active* versus *passive, subject* versus *object*? And can you see how this binary, scaled up to planetary size, this idea that is more than just an idea but an affective fantasy that structures how we conduct ourselves with relation to one another and with relation to nonhumans – can you see how this binary is part of the problem? We need to kick this Neo-platonic habit as soon as possible, the habit in which we are souls inhabiting bodies like captains steering ships or charioteers guiding chariots, in a world of objects that at best merely behave, either as manipulable lumps of stuff or as blank screens for the projection of our human-scaled desires.

If we're going to act collectively, at a species scale, in the name of the inevitable symbiotic solidarity we have with nonhuman beings, then we need a completely new idea of what "act" means that doesn't reproduce this binary. And this is what Tomás Saraceno's *Aerocene* project is helping us to imagine.

Some humans make a balloon. The balloon floats in the air. Some humans latch on to the balloon, holding it down with ropes while someone floats underneath it. The balloon reflects light. The balloon rides the air currents. The balloon feeds on the Sun. Humans photograph the balloon. And so on ... which of these verbs are examples of *acting* and which are examples of *behaving*?

An artist lets himself be seduced by the idea of making a sculpture as a balloon. He makes it, considering how it will float, tuning to the patterns of air flow and air pressure, the flow of heat and cold in the air, the cycling of sunlight and darkness. Is it active or passive, acting or behaving, when an artist makes something? When you speak, aren't you *listening,* in all kinds of ways, listening out for what your hearer needs, attending to her or his emotions (including not-attending to them), listening out for what you're going to say next? Are you acting or behaving? Is going-along-with a current situation, such as the air's heat or the brightness of the sun, simply passive, just being pushed and pulled by other things?

If the world is like that, we're going to need God again. We're going to need a prime mover to get all these inert components functioning in the first place. God gets to be the actor, the being who sets all the behavior in motion. Since a mechanism is merely moving, nothing is actually happening. There is no novelty. Nothing new can happen. Art is impossible. Creativity is impossible. Funnily enough, revolution is impossible. The idea that revolutionary action is the opposite of behaving – say blindly following an ideological code – is, strangely, exactly the wrong way to think revolution! You will never get "there" (acting freely to create a new world) from "here" (behaving as ideological puppets). Current revolution theories (for instance, theories of "the Event") are deeply religious in the precise sense of agricultural age theism, with its rigid binary of this world and the other world, soul and body, monarch and subjects, subjects and objects.

Strangely enough, we need to add a bit of so-called "passive" into the mix. A bit of an action, its quantum if you like, is more like what happens when we appreciate either as an artist making art, or as someone enjoying that art – after all, the artist is the first appreciator of her or his art, just like a writer is the first reader of her or his sentence. We need to think of ourselves as balloons who can float unsteadily on the currents of what is happening. I appreciate a silver balloon-like sculpture. It responds to the wind. Those things aren't that different. When you analyze it, action is made up of parts that are more like passion, appreciation, tuning… The "ground state" (as in quantum theory) of acting is a quivering vibration that we might call *stillness*, not a smaller bit of decisively-doing-something.

Saraceno is quite right to call *Aerocene* a "vision." This is not simply because it imagines a utopian future in which humans are more attuned to the biosphere in a non-violent way. It's also because, in its micro-structure, it imagines art as flashes of interactive appreciation, which when joined together look like "acting." And these "actions" are distributed between humans and nonhumans, in a spontaneously-emerging choreography. Someone gets inspired to fly a solar plane. The sun heats a balloon. The two are not so different.

The floating quality of *Aerocene* speaks to the openness, the "wiggle room" that this implicit new theory of action reveals. Since reality isn't a machine of perfectly interlocking parts, stuff can happen. And since "act" means "go along with" and not "cut into an inert continuum," we don't need to specify in advance or argue about who the "real," "actual" Actor (capital A) is: God, the state, history, will to power, spirit… All these imperialistic criminals are now disabled. Things can dance together, or not.

In turn this means that the differences between *act* and *play,* or *act* and *rehearse,* or *indicative* and *subjunctive* have also become strangely fuzzy. They haven't gone away completely. That would mean that everything is either totally passive or totally active: everything is God, everything is deadly serious, acting has been reduced to behaving. Isn't this seriousness a terrible gravity well for ecological art and action, which seems to be very keen to eliminate the playful, the delicate, in the name of amplifying *guilt,* that addictive substitute for thought that is an artifact of agricultural religion? And isn't the result the religious "unforgiveable sin" of despair? And if we curl up in the fetal position while the human species carries on extinguishing life on this planet, how come this is called being ecologically aware or philosophically astute?

What is the case is that things that seem inert, merely acted-on, non-human things, appear to be acting a little bit, while humans appear to be behaving a little bit more than we previously thought. Are we androids or not? Are we just an asteroid hurtling towards the nonhuman realm with unstoppable force or not? Are we objects or not? It is finally impossible to tell. That's what a person is: a being whose person-status is radically uncertain.

The pretense dimension of the word "act" (as in "theatrical actor"), has been restored. There is an illusory, ludic, tricksterish quality to how things work. We can never totally resolve in advance (or with hindsight, even) exactly what is happening. The Anthropocene happened precisely because of the elimination of the spooky, uncanny ties between *act* and *pretend, substance* and *accident.*

And this means that a genuinely "future future" is possible, not just a future we can extrapolate from existing affairs. *Aerocene* opens up this kind of future. It's an open-ended artwork about open-endedness, a *ballooning* artwork about our current age, but in such a way that this openness isn't in stark contrast to a static world. Rather, the openness of the future is achieved at all points – not in some impossible dimension removed from this physical world – in a wiggling, floating stillness. The balloon, with its childlike, playful connotations, is the perfect gathering-point for this open-ended dance of humans in solidarity with nonhumans, a space of attunement in which action and passion have blurred into one another. The reflective, silver sculpture blurs the difference between *reflect* or *appreciate* and *move* or *act*.

Moreover, isn't this exactly how to think solar energy? Visual art, looking and recording are all about light. But light isn't just an inert medium, it's an active set of things, a shower of photons. At the quantum level, *see* (or *measure*) and *change* become the same: a photon splashes onto an atomic particle and nudges it, changing its frequency. So in a solar age, an age where photons are how we organize our pleasures, such as flying and staying warm and cool, we must attune more to how *see* and *do* aren't as rigidly different as we thought.

Admiring a floating balloon. Saving the Earth from our extinction behavior. The two aren't so different.

Hans Ulrich Obrist (born 1968, Zurich, Switzerland) is Artistic Director of the Serpentine Galleries, London. Prior to this, he was the Curator of the Musée d'Art Moderne de la Ville de Paris. Since his first show World Soup (The Kitchen Show) in 1991, he has curated more than 300 shows.

Eva Horn is a professor of Modern Literature and Cultural Studies at the University of Vienna, Austria. She studied literature and philosophy in Germany and France. She taught at several universities in Germany, Switzerland, Austria and the US. Her research interests are political secrecy and conspiracy theory in modern fiction, disaster imagination in literature and art. Currently she is working on a cultural theory of climate. Besides numerous publications in German, she is the author of The Secret War. Treason, Espionnage, and Modern Fiction (Northwestern University Press, 2013), and The Future as Catastrophe (Columbia University Press, forthcoming 2018).

Tim Ingold (born 1948) is a British anthropologist, currently Chair of Social Anthropology at the University of Aberdeen. He was educated at Leighton Park School and Cambridge University. He is a fellow of the British Academy and of the Royal Society of Edinburgh. Ingold is researching and teaching today on the connections between anthropology, archaeology, art and architecture (the '4 As'), conceived as ways of exploring the relations between human beings and the environments they inhabit. Taking an approach radically different from the conventional anthropologies and archaeologies 'of' art and of architecture, which treat artworks and buildings as though they were merely objects of analysis, he is looking at ways of bringing together the 4 As on the level of practice, as mutually enhancing ways of engaging with our surroundings.

Timothy Morton is Rita Shea Guffey Chair in English at Rice University. He gave the Wellek Lectures in Theory in 2014 and has collaborated with Björk, Haim Steinbach and Olafur Eliasson. He is the author of Dark Ecology: For a Logic of Future Coexistence (Columbia, 2016), Nothing: Three Inquiries in Buddhism (Chicago, 2015), Hyperobjects: Philosophy and Ecology after the End of the World (Minnesota, 2013), Realist Magic: Objects, Ontology, Causality (Open Humanities, 2013), The Ecological Thought (Harvard, 2010), Ecology without Nature (Harvard, 2007), eight other books and 160 essays on philosophy, ecology, literature, music, art, architecture, design and food. Blog: http://www.ecologywithoutnature.blogspot.com. Twitter: @the_eco_thought

Tomás Saraceno's oeuvre could be seen as an ongoing research project, informed by the worlds of art, architecture, natural sciences, astrophysics and engineering. His floating sculptures, community projects and interactive installations propose and explore new, sustainable ways of inhabiting and sensing the environment. In 2009, he presented a major installation at the 53rd Venice Biennale, and was later awarded the prestigious Calder Prize. He has held residencies at Centre National d'Études Spatiales (2014–2015), MIT Center for Art, Science & Technology (2012–ongoing), among others. His work has been widely exhibited internationally in solo and group exhibitions.

<u>Acknowledgements</u>

I would like to extend my greatest thanks to all those
who worked and contributed to this book including
Eva Horn, Tim Ingold, Timothy Morton and Hans
Ulrich Obrist; designers Hendrik Schwantes and
Michael Heimann; Edoardo Ghizzoni from Skira and
members of Studio Tomás Saraceno including
Andrea Bagnato, Saverio Cantoni, Viola Castellano,
Connie Chester, Anna Garbuglia, Dario Lagana,
Ignas Petronis, Sophie Rzepecky and Raj Sandhu,
and for constantly supporting the studio - Dr. Martin
Heller and the representing galleries: Andersen's
Contemporary, Ruth Benzacar, Tanya Bonakdar,
Pinksummer Contemporary Art, Esther Schipper.

The Aerocene Foundation is a non-profit organization
devoted to community building, scientific research,
artistic experience, and education. Its activities are
manifested, among other things, in the testing and
dissemination of solar sculptures that float without any
need for fuel or for rare gases. The Foundation works
with artists, thinkers, scientists, researchers, balloonists,
technologists, humanitarian workers, and visionaries
to increase public awareness of global resource circulation, and reactivate a common imaginary towards new
symbiotic relationships with the earth. We are very
honored to work with many brilliant people around the
world. Please see the last page of Notes on Aerocene –
the visual essay within this book – for a short list of
collaborators. For a more extended list please visit:
aerocene.org/contributors